T0341582

THE UNIVERSITY OF MICHIGAN
CENTER FOR CHINESE STUDIES

MICHIGAN PAPERS IN CHINESE STUDIES

Ann Arbor, Michigan

TWO STUDIES ON MING HISTORY

by

Charles O. Hucker
Professor of Chinese and of History
The University of Michigan

Michigan Papers in Chinese Studies
No. 12
1971

*Open access edition funded by the National Endowment for the Humanities/
Andrew W. Mellon Foundation Humanities Open Book Program.*

Copyright 1971
by
Center for Chinese Studies
The University of Michigan
Ann Arbor, Michigan 48104

Printed and bound by CPI Group (UK) Ltd, Croydon, CR0 4YY


ISBN 978-0-89264-012-6 (hardcover)
ISBN 978-0-472-03811-4 (paper)
ISBN 978-0-472-12757-3 (ebook)
ISBN 978-0-472-90152-4 (open access)

The text of this book is licensed under a Creative Commons
Attribution-NonCommercial-NoDerivatives 4.0 International
License: https://creativecommons.org/licenses/by-nc-nd/4.0/

CONTENTS

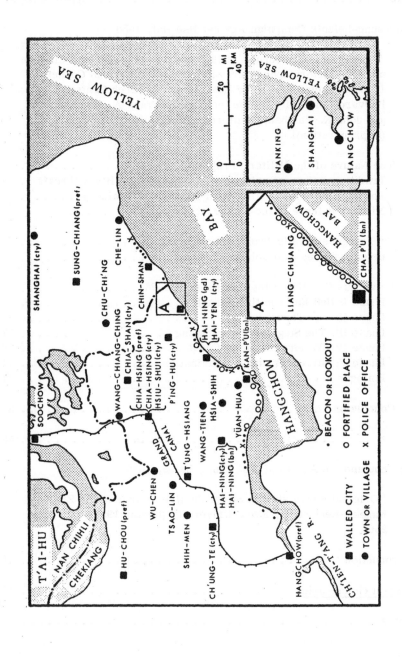

# HU TSUNG-HSIEN'S CAMPAIGN AGAINST HSU HAI, 1556

In the spring and summer of 1556 a renegade Chinese named Hsü Hai 徐海 led an invading group of Japanese and Chinese on a plundering foray through the northeastern sector of Chekiang province. Opposing them was a military establishment that for years past had been battered by coastal raiders, now under the control of an ambitious and clever civil official named Hu Tsung-hsien 胡宗憲 . In 1556 the raiders besieged cities and ravaged the countryside, defeated and terrorized the government soldiery in a series of skirmishes and battles, and accumulated booty and captives. Hu Tsung-hsien resorted to guile more than to force, turned the marauding leaders against one another, baited them with bribes and promises, and finally cleared the area of them. The campaign was not one of the most consequential in China's military history, even during the Ming dynasty (1368-1644). But it was famous and well reported in its time, and it illustrates some of the unusual ways in which the Chinese of the imperial age coped with the often unusual military problems they faced.

## 1. The Nature of the Military Problem

Traditional Chinese patterns of response to military threats. Over the preceding centuries the Chinese had grown accustomed to three major kinds of military challenges: (1) domestic disturbances created by discontented subjects, which at their strongest threatened and sometimes achieved changes of dynasties; (2) probing raids or occasional massive invasions of highly mobile northern nomadic peoples; and (3) resistance of southern and southwestern aboriginal tribesmen to the steady spread of Chinese settlement and sociopolitical organization. Against these potential challenges, both from within and from without, Chinese governments had come to put great faith in the suppressive influence of the awesome air of moral superiority that emanated from their sprawling civil officialdom. But behind the facade of self-righteous gentility there always were large armies in walled garrisons strung behind the Great Wall across northernmost China or spotted elsewhere at strategic points along important water and land routes. In face of all dangers, Chinese government policy fluctuated between two types of actions: (1) military initiatives to break up threatening confederations, to seize natural staging areas, or to keep the enemy off balance by shows of force; and on the other hand (2) diplomatic initiatives to mollify, threaten, cajole, confuse, or distract the enemy so that China's security was not likely to be endangered.

When hostilities erupted, whether on the frontiers or in the interior, the government traditionally considered two possible responses: (1) a straightforward military solution, called "extermination" (chiao 剿 or mieh 滅); or (2) an indirect politico-economic solution, called "pacification" (chao-an 招安, chao-fu 招撫, or similar terms suggesting "summoning and appeasing"), supported by real, but muted, threats of military action. In their pragmatic way, Chinese officials seem normally to have considered direct military solutions suitable only in the last resort, when the nation's vital interests were at stake and pacification was impossible or would yield unacceptable results. Except in the cases of notoriously bellicose Chinese leaders, pacification seems to have been greatly preferred as the normal means of coping with the disaffected. This preference no doubt reflects Chinese inclinations within the family and local community to "keep things going" at almost all costs, by mediating, compromising, and saving face all around.

The unprecedented challenge of Japan-based raiders. The Japanese were the first people who posed threats to China's security from non-contiguous territory.[1] Beginning in the early part of the thirteenth century, Japanese groups began raiding Korea; and after Khubilai Khan's unsuccessful punitive invasions of Kyushu in 1274 and 1281, they extended their raids to the coastal sectors of China. Strenuous diplomatic and defensive efforts by the early Ming emperors diminished the impact of these raids and channeled Sino-Japanese contacts into tribute-missions that were acceptable in the Chinese view of how foreign people should behave. But in 1548, following a series of disturbing tribute-mission incidents, these formal contacts were terminated.[2] Even before that time coastal raiding had been resumed on an ever increasing scale, and it reached and passed its peak in the 1550's. (This happened to be just the time when West European coasts, and especially shipping lanes, were being similarly harassed by marauders from the Barbary Coast of Africa.)

China's efforts to cope with these coastal marauders were complicated by several factors:

(1) There was the practical difficulty of trying to mount and maintain an adequate military defense along the entirety of China's long coastline.[3] The Ming rulers attempted to create a coastal equivalent of the Great Wall by establishing a line of walled cities,

small forts, stockades, watchtowers, and beacon mounds along the whole coast from Korea to Annam. Moreover, they maintained naval fleets that were supposed to patrol the estuaries, coves, inlets, and offshore islands that abound south of the Yangtze River delta. Since Ming naval ships were superior to the vessels used by the marauders and were normally victorious in open sea battles, Ming authorities realized it was better to catch raiders at sea than to track them down once they were ashore. But there was little confidence that even a strong coastal fleet would in itself guarantee security. To catch marauders fleeing outward laden with booty was one thing; to anticipate and fend off those who were approaching was another. However well defended, the China coast was extraordinarily vulnerable to raiding attacks.

(2) Denying the marauders their bases and staging areas would have required Chinese conquest and control of the Liu-ch'iu Islands, Taiwan, and even part of Japan itself. Early in the Ming dynasty, when the famous eunuch admiral Cheng Ho led huge armadas across the Indian Ocean, the establishing of an overseas Chinese empire might have seemed possible. Both T'ai-tsu (1368-1398) and Ch'eng-tsu (1402-1424) at least tried to intimidate Japan with threats of invasion. [4] But even these early Ming emperors were not foolhardy enough to carry out such threats, and later emperors had been so concerned about possible troubles in the north that they had allowed Chinese seapower to decline; so that no one could have suggested defense-by-conquest for serious consideration in the 1550's.[5] At the very time when Southeast China was most harassed by sea marauders, the attention of the court was particularly riveted upon the northern frontier, where Mongol power revitalized under Altan Khan was looming as the most serious military challenge China had faced in more than a century.[6] In 1550 Altan Khan plundered into the very environs of Peking, and thereafter until 1570 there were recurring alarms in North China and extraordinary expenditures to shore up the northern defenses. The 1550's consequently were not a time for risky adventurings of any sort in other areas.

(3) Moreover, the coastal marauding was by no means solely a problem in foreign relations. The marauders were generally called Wo-k'ou 倭寇 (Japanese Wako), "Japanese raiders," and it was the Japanese who had begun the raiding. But the Wako were never agents

of any organized Japanese government, and in the sixteenth century
(during most of which no effective central government existed in Japan)
raiding groups on the China coast generally included only small pro-
portions of adventuresome Japanese warriors. Even these were most-
ly led by Chinese renegades, and they were supported by other Chinese
renegades, offshore islanders, footloose mainlanders looking for pro-
fitable adventures, and sometimes, apparently, Portuguese and their
Malaysian hangers-on. By the 1550's, what the Chinese government
called Wo-k'ou constituted an international fraternity combining
smugglers who had now been badgered into marauding and their mainland collaborators, who even included persons of considerable local
and perhaps more far-reaching reputation and influence. The raiders
knew local conditions on the mainland, had excellent contacts in the
cities and towns, and were no doubt befriended and guided by local residents as effectively as were the government troops arrayed against
them. In short, there was no clearcut division between invading
"barbarians" on the one hand and a united local citizenry on the other.
As in the modern suppression of guerrilla insurgents, it was difficult
to plan for a decisive, direct military solution.

(4) The wealth and accessibility of the threatened area in the
1550's further complicated the problem. The focal area of Wako attack
in this period, the region traditionally called Chiang-nan ("South of the
River") or Tung-nan ("the southeast"), including the Shanghai-Soochow
portion of modern Kiangsu Province and the Hangchow-Ningpo portion
of Chekiang Province, has always been of strategic importance in
China's inter-regional and international relations. From T'ang and
Sung times on, Ningpo and Hangchow had been centers of international
trade, and in the early sixteenth century Ningpo was a center of
Portuguese activity in China. Eventually the sector became an important focus of British attention in the nineteenth-century Opium War,
when Chou-shan (Chusan) Island off Ningpo served as a major British
naval station, from which the British captured Ningpo, its guardian
city Ting-hai, and the excellent harbor of Cha-p'u near the northern
border of Chekiang. Ningpo and Shanghai were among the first treaty
ports opened to the Modern West; and Shanghai, of course, rapidly
became modern China's busiest port and most populous city.

This southeast China region was a natural target for the marauders of Ming times. Prevailing winds make it an easy voyage from Japan
to Chekiang in spring and autumn. The region is a plain crisscrossed by

waterways that make it easily penetrable by boats, and there are
innumerable excellent anchorages on its coast. It is (and in Ming
times was even more so) a densely populated region, intensively
cultivated and highly productive of both agricultural and manufactured
goods, inhabited by many rich and cultured families. In Ming times
it was the breadbasket from which grain taxes were shipped along the
Grand Canal from Hangchow northward to the capital at Peking and on
to the northern frontiers. For sixteenth-century marauders, it was
easy of access and bloated with potential plunder.

Military defense in the southeast through 1555. This whole region had been repeatedly victimized by marauders through the 1540's,
and the defense organization was therefore steadily strengthened.[7] In
1547 a Grand Coordinator (hsün-fu) had been assigned to Chekiang Province for the first time, with special jurisdiction over military matters
in the province and in the coastal prefectures of Fukien province to the
south. In 1554, after Hangchow prefecture had been seriously despoiled,
there was created in addition the post of Supreme Commander (tsung-tu)
of Nan Chihli (modern Kiangsu and Anhwei provinces), Chekiang, and
Fukien, which placed in one man's hands the responsibility of supervising defense against marauders throughout the whole southeastern
coastal sector. In the early 1550's many inland cities and towns of the
region, after being ravaged or threatened, were walled for the first
time in history.[8] To supplement the regular and militia forces of the
area, troops from distant parts of China were deployed into the Southeast, despite the concurrent drainage of troops from China's interior
to the northern frontier.[9] In 1555, as the military situation steadily
deteriorated, the court at Peking deputed the high-ranking Minister of
Works Chao Wen-hua 趙文華 (chin-shih 1529)[10] as a special Inspector
of the Armies in the Southeast. Soon the Supreme Commander Chang
Ching 張經 (chin-shih 1517)[11] was arrested and sentenced to death.
Grand Coordinator Chou Yün 周珫 (chin-shih 1532)[12] of the Nanking
area became the new Supreme Commander. After only one month in
office Chou Yün was dismissed, along with the Chekiang Grand
Coordinator Li T'ien-ch'ung 李天寵 (chin-shih 1538; later executed
together with Chand Ching).[13] The Vice Minister of Revenues at
Nanking, Yang I 楊宜 (chin-shih 1523),[14] became the third Supreme
Commander of the year; and Hu Tsung-hsien, then the Censorate's
low-ranking Regional Inspector of Chekiang, was given an extraordinary
promotion to succeed Li T'ien-ch'ung as Chekiang's Grand Coordinator.
Yang I was in turn dismissed in the second month of 1556, whereupon
Hu Tsung-hsien was made Supreme Commander. His former post as

Chekiang Grand Coordinator was soon filled by Yüan O阮鶚(1509-1567),[15] who had previously served as Education Intendant (t'i-tu fu-shih) in the province. By this time Inspector of the Armies Chao Wen-hua, after less than a year in the field, had returned to Peking full of assurances that the situation was at last under control.

By any reckoning, 1555 had been the most disastrous year in the long history of marauding in the Southeast.[16] Of Chekiang's eleven prefectures, only the three farthest inland -- Chin-hua centrally located, Ch'ü-chou in the far west bordering on Kiangsi province, and Ch'u-chou in the far southwest north of Fukien province -- seem to have been unscathed during the year. All of the six coastal prefectures-- from north to south: Chia-hsing, Hangchow, Shao-hsing, Ningpo, T'ai-chou, and Wen-chou--were violated, as were the two inland prefectures of Yen-chou southwest of Hangchow and Hu-chou northwest of Hangchow. The inland city of Ch'ung-te in Chia-hsing prefecture was occupied and looted. Fukien to the south, the Shanghai-Soochow region to the north, and even the north shore of the Yangtze River estuary were harassed. One group of bandits plundered westward up through inland Anhwei province to the very outskirts of Nanking, the Ming dynasty's auxiliary capital and a place of both strategic and symbolic importance.

Government forces had not been idle in the face of all this raiding activity in 1555, but they were not dramatically effective except in a few instances. The most successful government action was a sub-stantial victory at Wang-chiang-ching in northernmost Chekiang in the fifth month of the year, when raiders from a coastal base at Che-lin (north of Chin-shan Guard in Nan Chihli) were waylaid and slaughtered by a force under the ill-fated Supreme Commander Chang Ching, who was so soon to be executed for his failures. More than 1,900 marauders were reportedly beheaded in this action, thanks primarily to the utilization of newly-arrived aboriginal troops from Pao-ching and Yung-shun in the far northwestern sector of modern Hunan province, and thanks also to the leadership of veteran coast-defense generals such as Lu T'ang盧鏜 and Yü Ta-yu俞大猷(1503-1579).[17]

Marauding operations of 1555 in the crucial Soochow-Hangchow area were largely led by Hsü Hai, and it was his main force that suffered heavily at Wang-chiang-ching. Hsü had been a Chinese Buddhist monk originally associated with the ancient and famous Tiger Haunt Monastery

(Hu-p'ao ssu) outside Hangchow. Contemporaries often identified him by his Buddhist appellation, Ming-shan Ho-shang 明山和尚. How and when he became disaffected is not clear, but he seems to have won the respect of the marauders with his skills at divination and prognostication; they liked to call him "Generalissimo Commissioned by Heaven to Pacify the Oceans" (T'ien-ch'ai p'ing-hai ta chiang-chün). By the early 1550's he had reportedly become an associate of the most influential of all the marauder chiefs, another Chinese renegade named Wang Chih王直, the so-called "King of the Wako" ensconced in the Goto archipelago off Kyushu. Hsü's base was the Satsuma realm in southernmost Kyushu, and his main force consisted of Japanese from Satsuma and nearby realms including Izumi and Hizen. His exploits of 1555 established him as a marauder chief of the first magnitude.[18]

## 2. Hu Tsung-hsien: His Problems and Policies

Hu Tsung-hsien, who assumed responsibility for defense against the raiders in early 1556, was a native of Hui-chou prefecture in Anhwei province and a metropolitan examination graduate (chin-shih) of 1538.[19] He had served in two county magistracies in turn and had then been promoted to a post as investigating censor in the Censorate at Peking. After one censorial tour as regional inspector of the Hsüan-ta northern defense frontier, he appeared in Chekiang in 1554 in a similar role. He immediately became embroiled in the defense problems of the area and very quickly, as has been noted, rose to the exalted position of Supreme Commander.

Hu Tsung-hsien is generally described as a clever and ambitious man. From the first, his service in Chekiang got him involved in political relationships that were easily interpreted as opportunism on his part, which made him a highly controversial figure both in his own time and in the judgment of later historians. The times were complicated and the careers of all officials were difficult. The reigning emperor, Shih-tsung (1521-1566), got at odds with the officialdom at the outset of his reign in a famous "Rites Controversy" and had repeatedly shown inclinations to be cruel, capricious, and irrational. In the 1550's he was devoting himself to exotic Taoist exercises and leaving administration largely in the hands of his senior Grand Secretary, Yen Sung 嚴嵩
(1480-1565).[20] From 1542 to 1562 Yen Sung dominated the central government with the assistance of his notoriously corrupt son, Yen

Shih-fan嚴世蕃 (1513-1565); he has been held in contempt ever since as
a sycophantic, venal, and very self-seeking political manipulator.
Whether this judgment is fair or not, it was a fact of life in the 1550's
that one could accomplish little in government without enjoying the
favor of the Yens and helping to line their pockets.

Inspector of the Armies Chao Wen-hua appeared in Chekiang in
1555 as a protege of Yen Sung, so arrogant and avaricious that he was
probably more a hindrance than a help in the defense effort. Supreme
Commander Chang Ching and Grand Coordinator Li T'ien-ch'ung were
not appropriately deferential to Chao, to their ultimate undoing. But
Hu Tsung-hsien found (indeed, probably sought) favor with Chao and,
through Chao, with the Yens; hence he prospered. His power position,
however, was necessarily precarious. There were critics ready to
pounce on him at any opportunity and on any pretext simply because of
his association with Chao and the Yens; and pretexts were not hard to
find, whatever the military situation, because Hu could not survive
without "squeezing" his subordinates and the citizenry at large to
maintain a satisfactory flow of "gifts" to his patrons.

Thus the problems that Hu Tsung-hsien confronted in early 1556,
when Hsü Hai and his marauders reappeared in force, were multi-
faceted. He was very vulnerable to criticism for any mistake, as the
rapid turnover of his Supreme Commander predecessors made clear.
To avert personal disaster threatened by potential critics at court, he
must retain the good will of the Yens. To accomplish this, he must
avert military disaster; and to accomplish that, given the record of
successive disasters in prior years, he must be very clever indeed.
A resounding "extermination" of the marauders in a straightforward
military solution, however eagerly the government and the citizenry
alike might yearn for one, had repeatedly proved elusive even when
massive defense forces were assembled in the beleaguered Southeast
from far distant regions of China. "Pacification," on the other hand,
was not sure of acceptance either by the marauders or by the court.
On the northern frontier Altan Khan apparently could have been appeased from the first, as he was eventually, by the regularization of
frontier trading opportunities for the Mongols; but the court in the 1550's
was adamantly opposed to this. In the Southeast, the court's denial of
regularized trading opportunities to outsiders was the root of all the
coastal troubles; and the preeminent marauder chief, Wang Chih,
apparently could have been appeased at any time by a reversal of the

court's policy and amnesty for those who had violated it. Hsü Hai, for his part, seems to have been quite content with the existing situation, which had apparently yielded him enormous booty in 1555. He was not so likely to find any advantage in such terms even if they could be offered. Thus, although pacification tactics short of open-trade appeasement had been proposed and tentatively authorized as early as mid-1554, [21] such measures could be undertaken only at considerable risk.

There were at least three major risks: (1) Trying to "pacify" marauders, without enough military strength to fall back on, could expose the Southeast to military disaster. (2) "Pacification" attempts that proved less than wholly successful could expose Hu Tsung-hsien to charges of "giving free rein to bandits," which had already ruined some careers. (3) A determined "pacification" policy could further demoralize already badly demoralized subordinates, who consistently seemed convinced, no matter how disastrous the last battle had been, that the next battle would be a decisive victory. Hu Tsung-hsien's immediate civil-service subordinate, Grand Coordinator Yüan O, and his highest-ranking military-service subordinate, the Chekiang Regional Commander Yü Ta-yu, were particularly vocal arguers against appeasement. [22]

Despite all these recognized risks, Hu Tsung-hsien in 1555, while still Grand Coordinator, had persuaded his patron Chao Wen-hua that marauding could not be terminated by direct military means. On the pretext of spying on the marauders' bases in Japan and enlisting the cooperation of the Japanese authorities in marauder-suppression, he had dispatched a mission to the Goto archipelago to initiate negotiations with Wang Chih. The consequence of these negotiations is another important and intriguing story in itself, which culminated in Wang Chih's surrendering himself at Ningpo late in 1557. [23] What is immediately relevant here is the fact that Hu Tsung-hsien, throughout his 1556 campaign against Hsü Hai, was conducting negotiations with Wang Chih, using them to advantage in his dealings with Hsü Hai, trying to keep Wang Chih ignorant of the government's real intentions, and trying simultaneously to keep the court ignorant of promises he was making to Wang Chih. As events proved, Hu was an adept confidence man.

Before Hsü Hai's descent upon the Southeast in 1556, one of Hu

Tsung-hsien's envoys to Wang Chih had already returned from Goto accompanied by several raider chiefs, among whom was particularly included Wang's godson and intimate confidant, a Ningpo man known confusedly by the two names Wang Ao王漖 and Mao Hai-feng毛海峯. Hu's other envoys to Japan remained there more or less as Wang Chih's hostages; the formal excuse was that Japan was fragmented without a single ruler, so that Hu Tsung-hsien's proclamation to "the King of Japan" about marauder-suppression had to be taken slowly round to the regional lords in turn. Hu earnestly entertained Wang Ao in an effort to convince Wang Chih of his own sincerity, while the court was demanding that Wang Ao engage in some active marauder-suppression on his own part so as to demonstrate Wang Chih's good faith.

When Wang Ao made contact with Hu Tsung-hsien in Chekiang, probably very early in 1556, he reported (apparently with expressions of regret that Wang Chih could do nothing about the matter) that Hsü Hai and his Satsuma followers were preparing to strike the Southeast once more. In the second or third lunar month of the new year Hsü Hai did indeed land in the Cha-p'u region. From then until the eighth month of the year Hu Tsung-hsien was principally occupied with the immediate need to suppress Hsü Hai, even though dealing with Wang Chih and coping with Wako challenges elsewhere in his jurisdiction could not long be out of his thoughts.

Defense forces available in Che-hsi. The campaign against Hsü Hai stretched across the sector traditionally called Che-hsi, that portion of Chekiang that lies north of Hangchow and Hangchow Bay. The human resources that were available to Hu Tsung-hsien in that sector at the time can be considered in three categories of personnel:

(1) The first of these categories principally included the civil service officialdom of what might be called the normal administration. These were the prefects and prefectural staffs of Hangchow prefecture, of Hu-chou prefecture inland to the north, and especially of Chia-hsing prefecture to the northeast, which was the main theater of action; the magistrates of Chia-hsing prefecture's seven counties; the provincial-level executive officials of the Provincial Administration Office, the Provincial Surveillance Office, and the Chekiang Regional Military Commission; the Chekiang Regional Inspector delegated from the Censorate in Peking; and the Chekiang Grand Coordinator, equivalent to a provincial governor. The prefects and county magistrates had

residual responsibility for local defense and for this purpose maintained local militia forces; and both the Regional Inspector and the Grand
Coordinator had supervisory responsibilities concerning military
affairs in the province.

(2) The Chekiang Regional Military Commission had administrative
control over the regular military establishment of the province. [24] In
the Che-hsi sector this permanent establishment of hereditary officers
and soldiers included headquarters garrisons of three units of Guards
(wei): Hangchow Front Guard and Hangchow Rear Guard, both with
headquarters in Hangchow city, and Hai-ning Guard with headquarters
at Hai-yen county seat on the northeastern coast. Theoretically, each
such Guard comprised 5,600 hereditary regular troops and twenty-nine
officers of the hereditary military service. But by the middle of the
sixteenth century all Guards were notoriously understaffed. Moreover,
the Guard troops were actually deployed in fragments. Near-contem-
porary sources suggest that the normal complement of troops at Hai-
yen, for example, was 1,240. Battalion (so) units of undeterminable
strength, subordinate to the Hai-yen headquarters, were in flanking
walled garrisons to the south at Kan-p'u harbor and to the north at
Cha-p'u harbor. Another Battalion unit, detached from the Hangchow
Guards, was regularly stationed within the walls of Hai-ning county
seat between Hangchow and Kan-p'u. Other Guard troops, reportedly
in normal units of seventy, were assigned to each of six Police Offices
(Hsün-chien ssu) that were maintained in fortified places along the
coast by the civil service authorities of Hangchow and Chia-hsing
prefectures. [25] Yet other Guard troops must have been on detached
duty, in small platoons or squads, staffing other fortifications and
lookout stations that dotted the coast. One small fort was in the
environs of Hangchow city; there were five more clustered around
Kan-p'u, two near Hai-yen, and thirteen clustered between Cha-p'u
and Chekiang's northeastern border. Lookout stations were more
evenly scattered: six between Hangchow and Hai-ning, five between
Hai-yen and Cha-p'u, and nine between Cha-p'u and the northeastern
border. [26] Manning the walls and yamens of inland cities and towns
must have drained off still other regular troops from the Guard
garrisons. Even supposing that the three Guards in the Che-hsi sector
were near normal strength, so that ten or twelve thousand regular
troops were in the sector, the large majority of them -- and of the
irregular militia forces as well -- must have been immobilized in
these positional defense assignments, which could not safely be

abandoned. The number of troops who were normally available as a
mobile reserve must have been a relatively small proportion of the
total. Moreover, it is clear that the hereditary regular troops of the
Guards had long since deteriorated in quality to the point where they
could hardly be relied on even for positional defense. For the pursuit
and destruction of invading marauders, special forces were customarily
raised. [27]

(3) The third category of personnel available in Che-hsi might
appropriately be called the active tactical force. [28] It included civil
officials, military officers, and irregular troops. The Grand Coordinator and Regional Inspector of the province perhaps should be thought
of as belonging to this tactical group more than to the normal administrative hierarchy of the province. More particularly, one Vice
Commissioner (fu-shih) of the Provincial Surveillance Office was
specially assigned as circuit intendant of a Military Defense Circuit
(Ping-pei tao) covering Chia-hsing and Hu-chou prefectures, with
concentrated supervisory responsibility for all military matters in the
Che-hsi sector. The Che-hsi tactical group of military officers -- who
had rank status in the military administration hierarchy but were
detached for special duty -- principally included the Chekiang Regional
Commander (Tsung-ping kuan), who was the ranking field commander
in the province; a Regional Vice Commander (Fu tsung-ping kuan);
an Assistant Regional Commander (Ts'an-chiang) for Hangchow, Chia-
hsing, and Hu-chou prefectures, stationed at Hai-yen; and the Chekiang
Mobile Corps Commander (Yu-chi chiang-chün), stationed at Hangchow
city. The contingents of tactical troops that were commanded by these
officers were no doubt drawn in some part from the Guard garrisons
and militia units in the sector; but, probably more importantly, they
included specially-recruited local mercenaries (mu-tsu 募卒 ) and
military units assigned to Chekiang duty from outside the province. In
the Ming tradition, aboriginal tribes from central and southwestern
China were highly favored for such special deployment, although in
action against Wako marauders in the 1550's they had not proved wholly
reliable.

One contemporary source tells us that when Hu Tsung-hsien assumed his post as Supreme Commander in early 1556 he found that extra-
provincial forces borrowed from Szechwan, Hukuang (i.e. modern Hupei
and Hunan), Shantung, and Honan provinces at the request of his predecessors had been disbanded and sent home on the strength of Chao

Wen-hua's assurances to the court that coastal marauders were now under control; that his main force was three thousand mercenary recruits who were in such poor condition they were unfit for action; and that his only special reserves were one thousand aboriginal tribesmen borrowed from the Jung-mei area of modern Hupei province and eight hundred troops recruited in North China by the Mobile Corps Commander Tsung Li 宗禮 (1510-1566). [29] This reckoning probably does not include tactical forces who were nearby under the control of Regional Commander Yü Ta-yu and Regional Vice Commander Lu T'ang, both veterans of many coastal campaigns; nor does it take account of regular and irregular forces available in other sectors of Hu's jurisdiction, to the north in modern Kiangsu province and south of Hangchow Bay in Chekiang. For immediate marshalling against Hsü Hai within the Che-hsi sector itself, the tactical forces may have approached a total of ten thousand.

### 3. Hu Versus Hsü Hai in the Campaign of 1556

The many campaigns against marauders that were undertaken during the 1550's were abundantly recorded by participants and their contemporaries. The Wako problem attracted great attention at court, so that official chronicles of the era abound in relevant documents. Moreover, residents of the highly cultured Southeast, including such famous contemporary litterateurs as Kuei Yu-kuang 歸有光 (1506-1571) and T'ang Shun-chih 唐順之 (1507-1560), churned out essays and memoirs on the subject in even greater abundance, based on their personal experiences and observations. [30] Unfortunately, these source materials are of highly variable usefulness for understanding the wide sweep of events, and they are often frustratingly vague and contradictory about the dates and sequences of particular events. Later generations of Chinese and, eventually, Japanese historians have labored to produce reliable chronicles and analyses of the Wako crises, but without by any means solving all the problems even of simple chronology. [31]

The campaign against Hsü Hai in 1556 has not previously been studied in any detail, to the best of my knowledge, perhaps because the sources are peculiarly contradictory and confusing. In trying to pin down essential particulars of the campaign in the summary that follows, I rely primarily on two contemporary documents. One is specifically a narrative account of the campaign against Hsü Hai in

particular, by Mao K'un 茅坤 (1512-1601), a member of Supreme
Commander Hu's secretarial staff.[32] The other is a broader but
often more detailed chronicle of anti-Wako activities in the Che-hsi
sector from 1553 through 1556, by Ts'ai Chiu-te 采九德 , a resident
of Hai-yen, whose preface is dated 1558.[33] Combining data from these
documents in ways that seem to make sense and supplementing them
from the court's Veritable Records (Shih-lu) and similar sources[34]
gives us what I believe is a generally reliable understanding of Hsü
Hai's activities in 1556 and of Hu Tsung-hsien's campaign against him.
Since Hu Tsung-hsien's general strategy and capabilities required that
he leave the initiative to the invaders, the following phases are defined
by Hsü Hai's activities.

### Phase I:  Hsü Hai's Initial Assault

SUMMARY:  Apparently under the strategic direction of Wang
Chih in Goto, separate fleets of Wako raiders began landing in different
parts of the Southeast in the second lunar month of 1556.  One group
reportedly "several thousand" strong landed on the north bank of the
Yangtze River and began plundering Yang-chou and Chen-chiang
prefectures, threatening the heart of the Yangtze-Grand Canal waterways complex.  A second group of similar size landed on the south bank
of the Yangtze in the vicinity of Shanghai and began plundering inland
along the Wu-sung River. A third group of similar size struck to the
south of Hangchow Bay, in the Ningpo region.  These three relatively
small-scale invasions were soon reported to be diversionary efforts,
intended to draw attention and troops away from Che-hsi.  There Hsü
Hai himself, with a force of "more than ten thousand," hoped to subdue
the Hangchow area and then turn north to Hu-chou and the great city of
Soochow, and eventually to intimidate the dynasty's auxiliary capital,
Nanking.  Hsü Hai's force appeared in Cha-p'u harbor, easily destroyed
local naval forces that opposed them, smashed their own seagoing ships
as a symbol of their determination not to withdraw, and then moved
northward (presumably in small boats) around Chin-shan Guard to a
familiar raiders' haunt at Che-lin.  Hsü Hai was soon joined there by
other Satsuma-based raiders under the leadership of Ch'en Tung 陳東
and Yeh Ma 葉麻 (also referred to as Yeh Ming 葉明 and Ma Yeh 麻葉 ),
who had been plundering separately in the Shanghai region to the west.
In the third or fourth month these groups combined and moved southward to besiege the walled garrison at Cha-p'u but broke off the siege
after a week or so.  Meantime, supporting columns of raiders from

Che-lin and from the Shanghai area pressed inland to the vicinity of
Chia-shan.

*     *     *

When raiders first landed at Cha-p'u and to the north, Hu Tsung-
hsien had just assumed responsibility as Supreme Commander and was
apparently at his normal headquarters in Hangchow city. He alerted
all his subordinates to the danger and dispatched some of his forces
northeastward along the coast to Kan-p'u and Hai-yen. The defense
intendant of the Chia-hsing and Hu-chou circuit, Liu T'ao 劉燾 (chin-
shih 1538), apparently moved up the coast from his normal base at
Hai-yen to strengthen the walled garrison at Cha-p'u, and Grand
Coordinator Yüan O rushed toward Cha-p'u with what forces he could
rally in the Ch'ung-te area. Hu Tsung-hsien himself accompanied a
detachment northward from Hangchow into the Chia-hsing region,
whence he could move either northward to meet raiders of the Wu-sung
River area or eastward to close in on Cha-p'u. [35]

The first and most direct challenge came from the north, as raiders passed through the Chia-shan region toward the Chia-hsing
prefectural city. Hu, considering guile better than force in the circumstances, baited the raiders with a skiff loaded with more than a hundred
jugs of poisoned wine and manned by two reliable soldiers disguised as
troop-victuallers, who fled at first sight of the enemy vanguard.
Seizing the poisoned wine, the raiders halted and made merry. Some
died. By this time a detachment of "several thousand" newly-arrived
aboriginal tribesmen from Pao-ching in modern Hunan province had
joined Hu. They were anxious for a fight, and their chieftain, dis-
regarding Hu's cautions about the raiders' wiliness, led his men
straight into an enemy ambush. Hu rallied the survivors and set up
an ambush of his own, which mauled the advancing enemy sufficiently
to send him scurrying away northward toward Soochow. [36]

Already, in the third or fourth month, Liu T'ao was under siege
in Cha-p'u. Liu seems to have led his troops and the townspeople in
a gallant defense of the walls. Soon Hsü Hai, learning that both Hu
Tsung-hsien and Yüan O were converging on him, broke off the siege.

### Phase II: The Thrust Inland

SUMMARY: On withdrawing from Cha-p'u early in the fourth month, Hsü Hai moved his force inland. They overcame resistance offered by government troops from Hai-yen and Hai-ning, and for a time they plundered undisturbed in the Hsia-shih and Yüan-hua areas. In mid-month, now resigned to by-passing Hangchow, Hsü Hai moved on further inland to the northwest, reappearing to plunder the market towns of Tsao-lin and Wu-chen on the 18th and 19th days of the fourth month. Wu-chen is strategically located at the juncture of Hu-chou and Chia-hsing prefectures of Chekiang and Soochow prefecture of Nan Chihli to the north; in 1555 Hsü Hai had used Wu-chen as a base for harassing both the Hu-chou and the Soochow regions. Plundering through this sector again, his raiders on the 20th now encountered government forces near Tsao-lin. Three hard-fought battles followed in the region between Tsao-lin and Ch'ung-te, in which Hsü's forces were mauled and Hsü himself was wounded. But on the 23rd, when Hsü seemed on the verge of disengaging and fleeing in disarray, his scouts observed that the government forces were exhausted and without supplies and that no reinforcements were anywhere near; and in one more sharp encounter the raiders prevailed, slaughtering the government forces.

*         *         *

As soon as Hu Tsung-hsien's scouts reported that Hsü Hai's raiders were moving toward Wu-chen, Hu maneuvered to hem them in there. He ordered (a) troops from Soochow prefecture to move down to the north of Wu-chen, (b) waterborne troops of Hu-chou to move across to the west of Wu-chen, and (c) North China troops then at Chia-hsing to take up a defensive position near Wu-chen. With his own reserves of mercenary recruits and Jung-mei aborigines, he also moved cautiously toward Wu-chen. Grand Coordinator Yüan O simultaneously moved northward out of Ch'ung-te, en route picking up the North China troops that were moving westward from Chia-hsing under the control of Mobile Corps Commander Tsung Li.

It was Tsung Li and some nine hundred of his North China troops who came upon the much more numerous raiders near Tsao-lin and fought with them for successive days, eventually being almost totally massacred. Contemporary chroniclers called Tsung Li's struggle with Hsü Hai the most glorious example of a few standing heroically against a multitude in the whole history of warfare. [37] According to Mao K'un, Yüan O fled from the field after an initial skirmish. According to Ts'ai Chiu-te, Yüan O arrived in the vicinity only when Tsung Li's forces were already routed. Hu Tsung-hsien had at that time got no farther than Ch'ung-te in his progress toward Wu-chen.

During the fourth month, between Hsü Hai's departure from Cha-p'u and his victory at Tsao-lin, other Wako raiders were busy in other areas. North of Che-hsi, marauders plundered along the north bank of the Yangtze, ravaging Wu-wei county deep inland and the important grain depot at Kua-chou, where the Grand Canal "crosses" the Yangtze; and raiders kept active in the Shanghai area, finally being routed by the Chekiang Regional Commander Yü Ta-yu acting jointly with the defense intendant of the Soochow and Sung-chiang circuit, Tung Pang-cheng 董邦政. South of Che-hsi, raiders freely plundered the region between Hangchow and Ningpo, twice within one week sacking the Tz'u-ch'i county seat; and another group ravaged Wen-chou prefecture in southernmost Chekiang.

### Phase III: The Siege of T'ung-hsiang

SUMMARY: Victorious over Tsung Li but wounded and with a battered force, Hsü Hai pursued Yüan O to the walled city T'ung-hsiang where he understood there were tempting stocks of supplies. He laid siege to the city for approximately a month, using a variety of siege weapons including assault towers mounted on boats, a giant battering ram suspended in a wheeled scaffold, and a cannon of the type called "the general" (chiang-chün). But the city wall had been newly built in 1553 and was defended with imagination and verve by the county magistrate, Chin Yen 金燕 (chin-shih 1553). The marauders soon lost interest in costly assaults and settled down to starve out the city, meanwhile plundering freely in its environs. They became so inattentive that Grand Coordinator Yüan O was eventually able to slip out of the city by night and get away. The Wako leaders also became suspicious of one another. Hsü Hai and his powerful ally Ch'en Tung became so antagonistic that they finally broke off the siege and withdrew in separate directions, apparently between the 19th and 23rd days of the fifth month.

\*     \*     \*

When Hu Tsung-hsien, in Ch'ung-te, learned that Tsung Li's force had been massacred and that Yüan O was besieged in T'ung-hsiang, he was confronted with a difficult decision. Mao K'un tells us Hu considered the situation in the following terms:

> The North China troops have been beaten, and my own
> troops are so disheartened that they dare not fight.
> The Southeast is no longer manageable! Now the
> bandits have got T'ung-hsiang in trouble; but if I
> further divide up the forces they will ravage Ch'ung-te
> and ruin me as well (as Yüan O). It would be as
> if the two of us were to drown ourselves in each
> other's arms. What would become of the country
> then![38]

Deciding that caution was in order, Hu withdrew to his headquarters in Hangchow. But he made a show of organizing a relief expedition by ordering troops to converge around T'ung-hsiang: from Chia-hsing southward, from Hu-chou to Wu-chen, from Hai-yen to Wang-tien, and from Ch'ung-te to Shih-men.[39] He also ordered what remained of Tsung Li's North China troops to gather together at Ch'ung-te. Realizing that all these troops were badly demoralized by news of the Tsao-lin massacre, he also submitted to the court an urgent request for new contingents of aboriginal tribesmen from Pao-ching and Yung-shun in Hunan. Ignoring strongly worded, denunciatory appeals for help that were smuggled out of T'ung-hsiang by his besieged colleague Yüan O,[40] Hu decided that, while awaiting reinforcements, he would try the same pacification techniques on Hsü Hai that seemed to be working successfully on Wang Chih in Goto. Mao K'un cites Hu's arguments as follows:

> Even though (Wang) Chih and (Hsü) Hai are not of one
> mind about whether to submit or to resist, they are
> certainly as intimate as are lips with teeth. Once
> Chih has repented, can Hai alone not be persuaded with
> talk about his patriotic duty? If not, since he is an
> avaricious fellow, we can try luring him with baits and
> perhaps delude him. It seems to me that the T'ung-hsiang
> city wall, though small, is strong. If we delay for a
> few weeks, then the frontier forces of Yung (-shun) and

Pao (-ching) will arrive, and we can surely smash him.[41]

So Supreme Commander Hu began negotiating with Hsü Hai through intermediaries.

Hsü Hai, wounded and bogged down in an extended siege, was shaken by the news brought by Hu's agents that Wang Chih's godson Wang Ao had long since surrendered himself at Ningpo, bringing assurances that Wang Chih himself was preparing to accept pacification. (Before the T'ung-hsiang siege was ended, Wang Ao had even aided government troops to defeat Wako marauders who were withdrawing from the Tz'u-ch'i region south of Hangchow Bay.) Hu's agents persuaded Hsü Hai that his only hope of evading ultimate ruin was to cooperate similarly with the Supreme Commander. Hsü Hai argued that he was not alone and could not speak for his ally Ch'en Tung; but Hu's agents intimated that a separate agreement had been reached with Ch'en Tung, thus making Hsü Hai furiously suspicious of Ch'en. At the same time Ch'en was becoming equally suspicious of Hsü Hai as he learned that a series of government agents were visiting Hsü's camp. Hsü Hai eventually gave his word that he would surrender himself and accept pacification, on the condition that Supreme Commander Hu would provide substantive gifts with which Hsü might mollify his Japanese followers and would memorialize requesting that Hsü's offenses be pardoned. Hu Tsung-hsien was happy to comply with these terms. Negotiating agents carried great gifts of money and silks to Hsü Hai's camp outside T'ung-hsiang. Hsü Hai's messengers repeatedly expressed his gratitude, and as evidence of his good faith Hsü Hai handed over to the government some two hundred Chinese held captive by his men.[42] When he ultimately withdrew from T'ung-hsiang, he maliciously warned the defenders to beware of Ch'en Tung. Enraged upon finding himself thus abandoned by his ally, Ch'en Tung assaulted the city with new energy for one more day and then himself withdrew.

Meanwhile, when the court learned of the disaster at Tsao-lin and the siege of T'ung-hsiang, it ordered the calling up of troops from widespread areas of the country into a great expeditionary force for the Southeast, and on the eighth day of the fifth month Chao Wen-hua was once again dispatched to supervise activities there. On the 17th day, in response to Hu Tsung-hsien's request, six thousand tribesmen of Pao-ching and Yung-shun were ordered to hasten to join Hu's command.[43]

Phase IV: Withdrawal to the Coast

SUMMARY: When the marauders abandoned their siege of T'ung-hsiang late in the fifth month, they were heavily laden with plunder and seemed to have little heart for further hard campaigning. Ts'ai Chiu-te reports that their booty filled more than one thousand boats and that as they wound through the environs of Chia-hsing prefectural city their boats stretched out more than twenty Chinese miles (li).[44] This must have been one group alone, since it appears that Ch'en Tung and Yeh Ma made their way to a coastal camp at Hsin-ch'ang north of Che-lin in Nan Chihli, whereas Hsü Hai wound his way back through the Hsia-shih area.[45] His men set up separate temporary camps near Wang-tien, Yüan-hua, and Hai-yen, and he then gathered his forces together again near Cha-p'u, where Ch'en Tung and Yeh Ma soon rejoined him. There was some skirmishing while the raiders were returning to the coast. What was presumably the Ch'en Tung-Yeh Ma group, while passing through the Chia-hsing area, had an indecisive skirmish with a government force and lost twenty or thirty boats; and the Hsü Hai group fought off a Hai-ning Guard unit in the Hai-yen area.[46] When all of the marauders reassembled at Cha-p'u, early in the sixth month, antagonisms among the leaders became steadily worse, and they schemed against one another so viciously that only Hsü Hai remained at large by the end of the seventh month.

\*     \*     \*

During the marauders' winding withdrawals from T'ung-hsiang to the coast, some of Supreme Commander Hu's subordinates clamored to attack them in force. But Hu argued that available government troops were still so outnumbered that even a local victory might be disastrous to his over-all position. He insisted on pursuing his pacification tactics, taking advantage of rivalries among the marauder chiefs so as to bring about their submission peaceably. Hsü Hai had already accepted pacification in word though not yet in deed. Through intermediaries who made a succession of courtesy calls on the raiders' camps, Hu kept enticing Hsü with promises and urging him to give further evidence of good faith in the fashion of Wang Ao.

Wang Ao, after his previous foray in the Tz'u-ch'i area, continued to assist government forces to the south in the sixth month, subduing raiders on Chou-shan island and at Li-piao Bay, both in the Ningpo sector. Requested to assist in suppressing Hsü Hai, Wang Ao demurred, saying that only his godfather, Wang Chih, had sufficient authority for that. [47] Hu Tsung-hsien memorialized about Wang Ao's cooperation and requested that he be rewarded. The Ministry of War counseled the court that Hu should be allowed to use his own discretion in handling Wang Ao, adding, "In the practice of war one utilizes both spies and bait, sometimes summons (chao 招 ; peremptorily?) and sometimes mollifies (fu 撫). The important thing is to accommodate to changing situations and not be rigidly bound." [48] This advice was approved. Hu consequently issued gifts to Wang Ao on his own authority and sent him back to Japan to persuade his godfather to surrender himself.

The bait offered Hsü Hai and his allies was transportation. Hsü had burned his ships on arriving at Cha-p'u early in the year, and Ch'en Tung and Yeh Ma had been ashore even longer without access to sea-worthy vessels. All the marauders, with great accumulations of plunder, were now anxious about being marooned on the China coast with no hope of getting away with their booty. Hu Tsung-hsien realized this and made them a tempting offer. All who wished to surrender, he promised, would be welcomed and given status in the military establishment, whereas all who wished to return to Japan would be provided with seagoing vessels for the voyage. Although the marauders were by no means obtuse, as Ts'ai Chiu-te notes, they had virtually no choice but to make at least a show of cooperation. So on the 2nd day of the sixth month they sent word to Hu that his offer was accepted. [49]

Hu Tsung-hsien, apparently confident that Hsü Hai's will was broken, now began pressing him aggressively. He sent agents to point out that Hsü's fellow marauders in the Sung-chiang area to the north were bloated with spoils and were again heading inland. It was suggested that if Hsü Hai were to prove his sincerity by attacking the Sung-chiang raiders, he could have their spoils for himself and might even find some use for their boats. Hsü Hai, no doubt thinking he might in this way quickly get his hands on some seaworthy craft as well as some additional booty, complied. As he moved his forces westward to intercept the Sung-chiang group, Hu Tsung-hsien could not but realize that if Hsü Hai should renege on his promised cooperation and join forces with the Sung-chiang raiders for a drive southward into Che-hsi, the consequences would be disastrous. Hu had some misgivings, and no doubt several days of anxiety. But Hsü Hai kept his part of the bargain. He set upon the Sung-chiang raiders at Chu-ching north of the Chekiang border and routed them. To his dismay, however, most of his intended victims got away in the night with their boats and booty intact. Moreover, Hu Tsung-hsien had alerted Regional Commander Yü Ta-yu, who was lurking in the rear of the Sung-chiang group, to what was going on. While the marauder groups were fighting each other, Yü burned Hsü Hai's own river boats; and then, when the Sung-chiang survivors appeared on the coast fleeing seaward, Yü's fleet pounced on them and wiped them out.[50] Hsü Hai slunk back to his Cha-p'u harbor lair with an exaggerated conception of Hu's powers and thinking himself at Hu's mercy. He sent Hu elaborate gifts and reassurances of his obedience; he even turned over a younger brother named Hsü Hung as a hostage.[51]

At about this time Assistant Regional Commander Lu T'ang won a decisive victory over Wako raiders in T'ai-chou prefecture south of Ningpo after they had subdued the Hsien-chü county seat.[52] Thus with Chao Wen-hua approaching the Yangtze with an army ordered up by Peking and with marauders both north and south of Che-hsi having been dealt heavy blows, Hu Tsung-hsien was increasingly free to concentrate on Hsü Hai. He now plotted to persuade Hsü to betray and surrender his chief allies, Yeh Ma and Ch'en Tung.

It happened that Hsü Hai and Yeh Ma had already developed a sullen rivalry over a certain Mistress Chu (Chu fu 祝婦), a beauty whom Yeh Ma had taken captive at Yüan-hua and made his concubine. Hsü was also angry that Yeh Ma, who had accumulated the greatest quantity of booty among the chiefs, refused to agree to an equal division of spoils as the gang prepared to break up, some expecting to stay in China and some expecting to return to Japan when ships were provided. So Hsü Hai, at Hu's urging, arranged parleys with the prefectural authorities at Chia-hsing on the 26th day of the sixth month and again on the 3rd day of the seventh month to discuss the government's progress in gathering together the promised ships. Hsü got Yeh Ma to accompany him to these parleys, at which they were courteously entertained and given apologetic excuses for delays. Yeh Ma was so anxious to get out of China by this time, Ts'ai Chiu-te reports, that he was easily duped. On the second visit to Chia-hsing he got drunk and was taken into custody with no trouble.[53] A hundred or so of his followers, outraged at his capture but having no proof that Hsü Hai had betrayed him, soon gave Hsü by their conduct an excuse for taking them also into custody and turning them over to the government.

Supreme Commander Hu now pressed Hsü Hai to betray his more

powerful ally, Ch'en Tung. The fate of Yeh Ma naturally had deepened the distrust of Hsü that Ch'en had nursed since the siege of T'ung-hsiang, so that Ch'en was not to be so easily duped. Moreover, Ch'en had long been secretary or tutor of the younger brother of the Lord of Satsuma, Hsü's own patron; and the younger brother was apparently present as a member of the raiding party. Hsü Hai, while trying to keep Hu Tsung-hsien at bay with a show of cooperation, was by no means happy at the prospect of spoiling his relations with the Japanese. So he was most hesitant to make an overt move against Ch'en Tung. The Supreme Commander, understanding his difficulty, began sending agents with beautiful trinkets for two of Hsü's favorite mistresses, enlisting their aid in his campaign to urge Hsü to action. Hu also made use of the captured Yeh Ma, who no doubt happily wrote a letter to Ch'en Tung, at Hu's suggestion, explaining Hsü's treachery and urging Ch'en to destroy him. Hu saw to it that the letter was put in Hsü's hands rather than Ch'en's. This served two purposes. Not only did it infuriate Hsü Hai to the point of determining that he must get rid of Ch'en; it also led him to believe that Hu was genuinely befriending and protecting him, and that he consequently owed Hu a great debt of gratitude.

At this juncture, on the 6th day of the seventh month, Chao Wen-hua arrived in Chia-hsing, and units of his expeditionary force soon began taking up positions in the sector between Chia-hsing and the coast. Grand Coordinator Yüan O, who since escaping from the siege of T'ung-hsiang had been conducting defensive operations south of Hangchow Bay, now also brought his forces into Chia-hsing. Hsü Hai was increasingly overawed by the dignitaries arrayed against him even though Hu and Chao, for their part, were not yet sure they had enough strength for an attempt at straightforward extermination. Hu could not expect to protract his pacification tactics much longer without exposing himself to severe criticism. So one of Hu's negotiating agents was sent to Hsü Hai with a message from Chao:

> If you bring in your forces for submission you may
> escape the death penalty. But if you do not present
> Ch'en Tung in custody together with a thousand or
> so severed heads (of his supporters) I fear I shall
> not be able to appease the court. If you are able to
> do this, then I will join the Supreme Commander in
> memorializing for your pardon. Otherwise, you
> will be pounded into powder. [54]

In desperation, Hsü Hai now gathered up booty worth "more than a thousand gold" taels and sent it to Ch'en Tung's patron, the younger brother of the Lord of Satsuma, asking permission to borrow Ch'en's services. When Ch'en appeared, Hsü managed to get him delivered into government hands, no doubt by deception. Hsü now realized he could never safely return to Japan, and he knew that Ch'en Tung's supporters would murder him at any opportunity.

Hu Tsung-hsien pressed his psychological advantage ever more strongly. He now sent a personal message to Hsü Hai:

> I want to be lenient with you, but Minister Chao considers
> your crimes to be truly heinous. Why not heed me?
> Several tens of ships are moored on the coast. If you
> rally (Ch'en Tung's followers) to make a rush for
> these ships on the coast (with the consequence that )
> a thousand or so can be captured for presentation to
> Chao, you might thereby save yourself. [55]

As Mao K'un observes, Hsü Hai might have been reluctant, but he had no alternative. [56] So he came to an agreement with circuit intendant Liu T'ao, stationed at Hai-yen. Government ships were indeed moored in Cha-p'u harbor, while Liu T'ao concealed a large force of government troops inside the Cha-p'u walls. Announcing that the long-promised government ships were at last available, Hsü Hai shepherded the whole marauder host onto the Cha-p'u beach, carefully restraining his own followers. When the others were scrambling gleefully for the ships, at a signal from Hsü Hai, Liu T'ao led his forces out of the walled garrison and slaughtered the disorganized mob. Those who managed to get aboard the ships were quickly rounded up by a naval squadron waiting for them. The marauder lair at Cha-p'u harbor was totally laid waste, and Hsü Hai crept away to a new camp at nearby Liang-chuang to work out the best fate he could. [57] It was now the end of the seventh month.

### Phase V: Surrender and Extermination

SUMMARY: Having fulfilled all the tests of sincerity that had been imposed on him, Hsü Hai demanded that his surrender be accepted, and on the first day of the eighth month he and a hundred or so of his followers appeared for audience with the provincial authorities in P'ing-hu county seat. He was politely received and was temporarily allowed to take up residence in an estate near the city. There Hsü eventually realized that he had been totally deceived, and he tried to rally new support among his Chinese neighbors. But he was now surrounded by overwhelming government forces, which on the 25th and 26th days of the month assaulted and destroyed both his temporary camp and the lair at Liang-chuang near Cha-p'u. Hsü Hai drowned himself in a stream.

\*        \*        \*

When the Wako raiders had been decimated in Cha-p'u harbor and Hsü Hai had settled at Liang-chuang, Hsü asked permission to present himself in formal surrender at P'ing-hu, and it was agreed that he should do so on the second day of the eighth month. Inspector of the Armies Chao Wen-hua, Supreme Commander Hu Tsung-hsien, Grand Coordinator Yüan O, and Regional Inspector Chao K'ung-chao 趙孔昭 (chin-shih 1544) all gathered at P'ing-hu to receive him. To the annoyance of these dignitaries, Hsü appeared one day early, deployed his whole force outside the city, and demanded that he be admitted with a hundred or so of his men in full armor. Marshaling a strong show of military force along the streets of the city, but with misgivings nevertheless, the dignitaries consented. Assembling on a dais in the county yamen, they gave him audience in a remarkable scene vividly described by Mao K'un as follows:

> (Hsü) Hai and his warriors faced north toward the four
> dignitaries and in succession kowtowed and cried, "O
> star in the firmament, we deserve death; we deserve
> death!" (Hsü) Hai wanted to pay special respects to
> Hu (Tsung-hsien) but did not know him by sight. So he
> glanced for guidance to the intermediary agents, who
> signaled him with their eyes. (Hsü) Hai then faced
> Hu once more, kowtowed, and cried, "O star in the
> firmament, I deserve death; I deserve death!" Hu
> thereupon descended from the dais, patted (Hsü) Hai
> on the head with his hand, and said to him, "You have
> distressed the Southeast for a long time! Now that
> you have at last submitted, the court will pardon you.
> But be sure not to make any further trouble!" (Hsü)
> Hai again kowtowed and cried, "O star in the firmament,
> I deserve death, I deserve death!" Then the four

> dignitaries handed out generous gifts, and (the
> visitors) departed. [58]

Ts'ai Chiu-te describes the scene in almost identical terms but adds
that Regional Inspector Chao K'ung-chao could not control his indignation
and shouted at Hsü, "You have slaughtered our people beyond counting.
What punishment you deserve!"[59]

By this time the whole expeditionary force brought from the north
by Chao Wen-hua and local forces under the control of Regional Commander Yü Ta-yu and Regional Vice Commander Lu T'ang were all in
position in Che-hsi. But the authorities in P'ing-hu were still wary of
Hsü Hai. "They calculated that he still had more than a thousand men
under his command," Mao K'un relates, "and they were so fierce and
violent that it would be difficult to crush them."[60] Moreover, it
would still be a while before the six thousand tribesmen coming from
Pao-ching and Yung-shun could be expected to arrive. So they invited
Hsü Hai to choose a campsite where he could wait comfortably while,
presumably, they pleaded his case at court. He remembered having
been impressed, during previous raiding visits, by a so-called "Shen-
family estate" (Shen-chia-chuang 沈家莊) outside the city,[61] and they
rented it for him. Hsü Hai settled there on the 8th day of the month.
He even suggested that once his pacification was regularized, he would
like to buy the estate and three thousand nearby acres (mou) of
agricultural land.[62] Hu Tsung-hsien persuaded him to encamp remnants
of Ch'en Tung's raider group alongside his own, assuring him that
"government troops will protect you against the (Ch'en) Tung gang;
don't be afraid."[63]

Ts'ai Chiu-te reports that Hsü Hai was not yet resigned to a
disastrous fate. On the 11th and 12th days of the month he invited
Chinese residents of his neighborhood to wine-drinking parties, and he
thus enticed two or three hundred young men to join him afresh. Somewhat emboldened, he rebuffed an invitation from the authorities in
P'ing-hu to attend a moon-watching party on the 15th, and on the 17th
he went so far as to detain and decapitate an envoy from Hu Tsung-
hsien.[64] Hu, for his part, was daily sending agents to urge on the
approaching troops from Pao-ching and Yung-shun; and when Hsü Hai
sent him two hundred gold taels for the purchase of wine Hu arranged
for the wine to be delivered contaminated with poisonous drugs.[65]

The Pao-ching and Yung-shun tribesmen apparently reached P'ing-hu on the 20th, and peripheral skirmishing began in the area of Hsü Hai's encampment. The government forces seem to have been none too eager for the culminating assault. So Hu persuaded his captive Ch'en Tung to write a letter to his former followers warning them that Hsü Hai was collaborating with the government forces in a plan to crush them in a pincers operation. This provoked a clash between Hsü Hai's group and the Ch'en Tung group during the early morning of the 25th, in which Hsü Hai was wounded; and on the 25th and 26th government forces moved in decisively on all sides. All marauders in the Shen estate were wiped out, and Regional Commander Yü Ta-yu also destroyed remnants in the camp at Liang-chuang. Hsü Hai's drowned body was found in a stream, and it was decapitated. It is reported that from 1,200 to 1,600 raiders were decapitated in all.[66]

In subsequent mopping-up operations, Regional Vice Commander Lu T'ang pursued and captured a Japanese named Shingoro, whom Hsü Hai had dispatched from the Shen estate to find his way to Japan; and during the following winter Regional Commander Yü Ta-yu cleared Chou-shan island to the south of the Wako remnants in refuge there.

Reports of the victories in the P'ing-hu region from Chao Wen-hua and Hu Tsung-hsien reached the court at Peking on the 19th day of the ninth month. Congratulations and promotions were ordered; and on the 27th day sacrificial reports of the extermination of Wako marauders in the Southeast were made in ceremonies at the imperial altars and temples in Peking.[67] The prisoners Yeh Ma, Ch'en Tung, Hsü Hung, and Shingoro, and the severed head of Hsü Hai were all subsequently displayed in imperial audience,[68] and in the twelfth month of the year the prisoners were executed.

Epilogue. The campaign against Hsü Hai in 1556 was by no means the end of China's troubles with Wako marauders, but it did terminate the worst of the plundering in the Southeast. In 1557, by means of equally complicated and intriguing negotiations, Hu Tsung-hsien disposed of Wang Chih. Thereafter the Wako raiders were less well organized, and they usually by-passed Nan Chihli and Chekiang to raid southward in Fukien and Kwangtung provinces.

Hu Tsung-hsien remained in power in the Southeast and in imperial favor despite the successive ruin of his patrons Chao Wen-hua in 1557 and Yen Sung in 1562; but he was repeatedly denounced for corruption and abuse of authority. At the end of 1562 he was relieved of duty and taken to Peking to answer such charges. The emperor defended him as a loyal and effective official, and he was allowed to retire more or less honorably. Denunciations continued, and in 1565, despite the emperor's continuing sympathy for him, he was sent to prison, where he died of ill treatment.[69]

The official history of the dynasty, the Ming-shih, says of Hu: "Tsung-hsien suffered disgrace because of his extravagance and defilement. But if he had permitted the scoundrels Hsü Hai and Wang Chih to evade death, how much more trouble would have occurred can only be guessed."[70] Other historians have similarly found it necessary to overlook his shortcomings. The editors of the great eighteenth-century imperial catalogue Ssu-k'u ch'uan-shu tsung-mu insisted that he should not be belittled. "Although he was not an ideal man," they judged, "his abilities certainly made him one of the heroes of the age."[71]

## 4. Conclusion

The history of Hu Tsung-hsien's campaign against Hsü Hai in 1556 has relevance to an almost unlimited range of important scholarly problems. Among these are problems concerning the socioeconomic development of China's Southeast, Sino-foreign and especially Sino-Japanese relations, Japan's relations with the outside world in general and Japan's own economic and cultural development in the sixteenth century, conditions of service generally in China's traditional government, and the political climate and history of Emperor Shih-tsung's reign, in addition to multi-faceted problems concerning traditional China's military history and institutions in particular.

This paper is hardly the place to pursue all these varied ramifications, but it might not be amiss to close here with some brief comments on the nature and exercise of Hu's authority as a commander. In his valuable recent article, "Policy Formulation and Decision-Making on Issues Respecting Peace and War," Professor Jung-pang Lo has demonstrated conclusively that important decisions arrived at by the Ming court were not dictated according to "the whim and caprice of any single individual."[72] His study can be usefully supplemented by evidence from the 1556 campaign about military decision-making on lower levels, regionally and locally.

One thing immediately apparent is that Supreme Commander Hu was in no sense a regional warlord of the modern type. He was subject to the court directly and through such intermediary agents as Chao Wen-hua. Moreover, although this aspect of the situation is not explicitly shown in the foregoing narrative, his relationship with the court was vulnerable to harassment through means that by-passed the normal chain of command -- for example, through personal contacts at court that could be exploited by his subordinates and by influential personages of Chekiang. He was also plied with advice by friends and acquaintances, which at any time could have been transformed into sharp criticism poured into receptive ears at court.

But it is equally apparent that Shih-tsung and his court made few specific demands on Supreme Commander Hu as regards the Wako troubles. They wanted the troubles terminated, and they ruled full pacification out of consideration as an acceptable means. But Hu was authorized, implicitly and explicitly, to achieve his goal by tactical decisions made at his own discretion (pien-i 便宜 ).

The pattern of events in 1556 suggests that it was tactically important to Hu Tsung-hsien that Hsü Hai should at all times believe Hu to have great military force at his disposition, and that Hsü at certain times should believe Hu to be his friend. When Hu in fact lacked the resources to be militarily aggressive he unhesitatingly resorted to bribery, courteous exchanges of messages, promises of official status and even of ships, friendly albeit false warnings of plots on the part of Hsü's colleagues, and even cordial personal receptions; and he consistently avoided decisive military confront-ations. On the other hand, when circumstances warranted, Hu attempt-ed to poison the enemy, connived with Hsü's colleagues and mistresses against him, coercively tricked Hsü into unpalatable and disadvantageous undertakings, and made threatening shows of force. Moreover, as the military situation altered in his favor Hu became increasingly belligerent, and in the end he organized and led a military extermination of Hsü.

Except for the final extermination of Hsü Hai, none of Hu Tsung-hsien's tactical maneuvers was specifically sanctioned by the court or its agents. Moreover, for the most part, they seem not to have been supported eagerly by his subordinates. Decisions were made by Hu in response to the changing situations that confronted him. He made them in consultation with his subordinates, but he made them on his own authority and with full and heavy responsibility for them. It was no doubt gratifying to him that military extermination ultimately proved to be possible. But the evidence makes it reasonably clear that if non-military pacification had proved to be politically acceptable, as well as possible, Hu in his pragmatic way would just as gladly have pursued his pacification (i.e., appeasement) tactics.

A similar sense of being free to act at one's own discretion seems to have characterized Supreme Commander Hu's subordinates. It is perhaps not surprising that the local authorities at Cha-p'u and at T'ung-hsiang apparently acted on their own initiative and with self-reliance when they were besieged and isolated. It is worthy of note, however, that Grand Coordinator Yüan O reportedly departed from Ch'ung-te to go to the aid of beleaguered Cha-p'u without waiting for Hu's orders;[73] that Mobile Corps Commander Tsung Li apparently took the initiative in engaging Hsü Hai near Tsao-lin without having orders from Hu to engage him; and that even in the coordinated final assault on Hsü Hai, Regional Commander Yü Ta-yu seems to have acted with a substantial degree of independence. It is perhaps less surprising, but no less suggestive, that the leader of the aboriginal tribesmen from Pao-ching reportedly disregarded the Supreme Commander's cautions about engaging the marauders in the Chia-shan area, to the tribesmen's regret. [74] In the same degree that Supreme Commander Hu took action at his discretion when he had no contrary orders from the court or its agents, so his subordinates, sometimes even in his presence, apparently took such action as they deemed appropriate.

It might be argued that the independence displayed by these various field commanders suggests, not only that they were free of unreasonable constraints imposed from above, but also that there was a real lack of discipline among them. It must be kept in mind, however, that the nature of the Wako threat was well understood, both locally and at court; and coping with it successfully no doubt required a degree of independence at all command levels that might have been wholly inappropriate in other circumstances. Whatever this analysis of the 1556 campaign may suggest in this regard, it would probably be premature to conclude that Ming armies in the field were characteristically assemblages of quasi-independent command units.

It might be noted, finally, that in achieving his goal Hu Tsung-
hsien seems to have been remarkably free of moralistic inhibitions,
whether externally imposed or self-developed. His mandate was to
get rid of Hsü Hai, and he did so with what seems like very little regard
for considerations of propriety, integrity, or either personal or national
honor. Surviving and winning was his mission as he conceived it; and
it is apparent that Shih-tsung shared Hu's conception, for the emperor
never seriously wavered in his judgment that Hu was a loyal and
effective official. Such things should not be disregarded in our continuing efforts to assess the national military style of traditional China.

NOTES

General: Names of government agencies and official titles are
rendered in accordance with the system set forth in my article
"Governmental Organization of the Ming Dynasty", in Harvard Journal
of Asiatic Studies, vol. 21 (December, 1958), pp. 1-66; and its index
of terms and titles, published in Harvard Journal of Asiatic Studies,
vol. 23 (1960-1961), pp. 127-151. Both article and index are reprinted
in Studies of Governmental Institutions in Chinese History (John Bishop,
ed.: Cambridge, Mass., 1968).

1. It will be clear to any specialist that I have not exhausted all
sources that relate to the campaign of 1556, much less all sources that
relate to the Wako problem of Ming times more generally. An excellent
discussion of Chinese works of Ming times that bear on the Wako
problem is Wu Yü-nien's article "Ming-tai Wo-k'ou shih-chi chih-mu,"
reprinted in 1968 in volume 6, pp. 231-252, of Ming-shih lun-ts'ung,
edited by Pao Tsun-p'eng; and an up-to-date bibliography of relevant
Japanese materials is provided in Tanaka Takeo's small volume, Wako
to kango boeki (Tokyo, 1961). A documentary chronicle of Wako
activities and defense against them throughout Chinese history is Wang
P'o-leng's Li-tai cheng-Wo wen-hsien k'ao (Cheng-chung shu-chü, 1940).
Li Kuang-ming's Chia-ching yü-Wo Chiang-Che chu-k'o chün k'ao
(Yenching Journal of Chinese Studies, Monograph Series No. 4, 1933);
Ch'en Mao-heng's Ming-tai Wo-k'ou k'ao-lüeh (same series No. 6,
1934); Wu Ch'ung-han's Ming-tai Wo-k'ou fan-hua shih-lüeh (Ch'ang-
sha, 1939); Li Kuang-pi's Ming-tai yü-Wo chan-cheng (Shanghai, 1956);
Ch'en Wen-shih's Ming Hung-wu Chia-ching ti hai-chin cheng-ts'e
(Taipei, 1966); and Ch'en's article "Ming Chia-ching nien-chien Che-
Fu yen-hai k'ou-luan yü ssu-fan mao-i ti kuan-hsi," in Bulletin of the
Academia Sinica Institute of History and Philology, vol. 36, part 1
(1965), pp. 375-418, are all useful works of modern Chinese scholar-
ship on the subject. A. Tschepe's Japans Beziehungen zu China seit
den Altesten Zeiten bis zum Jahre 1600 (Jentschoufu, 1907) is a surpris-
ingly detailed chronicle of reference value, but without citations of
sources. Relevant modern works in Western languages especially
include Y. S. Kuno's Japanese Expansion on the Asiatic Continent
(2 vols.; Berkeley, 1937-1940); Wang Yi-t'ung's Official Relations
Between China and Japan, 1368-1549 (Cambridge, Mass., 1953);
Bodo Wiethoff's Die chinesische Seeverbotspolitik und der private

34

Überseehandel von 1368 bis 1567 (Hamburg, 1963); Benjamin H. Hazard's "Japanese Marauding in Medieval Korea: The Wako Impact on Late Koryo" (Ph. D. dissertation, University of California at Berkeley, 1967); Hazard's article "The Formative Years of the Wako, 1223-63," in Monumenta Nipponica, XXII (1967), 260-277; and James F. Millinger's "Ch'i Chi-kuang, Chinese Military Official" (Ph. D. dissertation, Yale University, 1968).

2. Wang Yi-t'ung, p. 80.

3. Standard map-studded sources on Ming coastal defenses are Cheng Jo-tseng's Cheng k'ai-yang tsa-chu (Photolithographic reprint, 1932) and Ch'ou-hai t'u-pien (1624 ed.is cited hereinafter), attributed to Hu Tsung-hsien but undoubtedly also the work principally of Cheng Jo-tseng. Cf. Wolfgang Franke's An Introduction to the Sources of Ming History (Singapore, 1968), pp. 223-224; and Wang Yung, "Ming-tai hai-fang t'u-chi lu," reprinted in volume 6 of Ming-shih lun-ts'ung, pp. 205-230.

4. Wang Yi-t'ung, pp. 10, 16-17, 48, 50.

5. On the deterioriation of Ming naval power, see the stimulating interpretive article by Lo Jung-pang, "The Decline of the Early Ming Navy," in Oriens Extremus, V (1958-59), 149-168.

6. See the biography of Altan Khan by Henry Serruys and Fang Chao-ying in Draft Ming Biographies (published by the Association for Asian Studies, Inc.), no. 1 (1964).

7. A general discussion of Ming coastal defense organization can be found in Ming-shih (Po-na ed., 1940), 91.10a ff. More specific data on defense organization in Chekiang is in Ch'ou-hai t'u-pien, 5.8a-17b; and particularly in Fan Lai et al., Liang-Che hai-fang lei-k'ao hsü-pien (8-chüan ed. dated 1602), especially chüan 2. Cf. Wolfgang Franke, p. 227; and Wang Yung, pp. 212-213.

8. Ch'en Mao-heng, pp. 139-142.

9. Li Kuang-ming, passim; and Ch'en Mao-heng, pp. 151 ff.

10. See the biography of Chao Wen-hua in Ming-shih, 308.17b-21a.

11. See the biography of Chang Ching in <u>Ming-shih,</u> 205.4a-6a.

12. See the biography of Chou Yün in <u>Ming-shih</u>, 205.6b-7a.

13. See the biography of Li T'ien-ch'ung in <u>Ming-shih</u>, 205.6a-b.

14. See the biography of Yang I in <u>Ming-shih</u>, 205.7a-b.

15. See the biography of Yüan O in <u>Ming-shih</u>, 205.13b-14a.

16. Chronological charts of Wako activities in 1555 are provided in <u>Ch'ou-hai t'u-pien,</u> chüan 8; and Ch'en Mao-heng, pp. 78-81. Cf. Wu Ch'ung-han, pp. 63 ff.

17. See the biographies of Yü Ta-yu and Lu T'ang in <u>Ming-shih</u>, 212.1a-9b; and the biography of Lu T'ang by Bodo Wiethoff in <u>Draft Ming Biographies</u>, no. 6 (1966). For the victory at Wang-chiang-ching see Hsia Hsieh's <u>Ming t'ung-chien</u> (reprinted ed., 1959), chüan 61 (vol. 3, pp. 2336-2337); Wang P'o-leng, p. 189; Wu Ch'ung-han, p. 58; and <u>Ch'ou-hai t'u-pien</u>, 9.2a-3b.

18. On the life of Hsü Hai, see Ch'en Mao-heng, pp. 103-104; and Ku Ying-t'ai, <u>Ming-shih chi-shih pen-mo</u> (Wan-yu wen-k'u ed.), chüan 55 (section 8, pp. 54-55). On Wang Chih, see Ch'en Mao-heng, pp. 102-103; Ch'en Wen-shih, "Ming Chia-ching nien-chien Che-Fu yen-hai k'ou-luan yü ssu-fan mao-i ti kuan-hsi," pp. 395-405; Tanaka Takeo, pp. 200 ff.; Bodo Wiethoff, <u>Die chinesische Seeverbotspolitik und der private Überseehandel von 1368 bis 1567,</u> pp. 188 ff.; Fu Wei-lin, <u>Ming-shu</u> (reprinted ed., 1937) chüan 162, pp. 3213-3217 (a biography of Wang Chih, reprinted in its entirety in Wang P'o-leng, pp. 209-214); and <u>Wang Chih chuan</u>, an early biography reprinted in <u>Hsüan-lan-t'ang ts'ung-shu hsü-chi</u> (1947), volume 15, and virtually identical with a narrative entitled <u>Ch'in-huo Wang Chih</u> found in <u>Ch'ou-hai t'u-pien,</u> 9.24a-29b.

19. See the biography of Hu Tsung-hsien in <u>Ming-shih</u>, 205.8a-14a.

20. See the biography of Yen Sung in <u>Ming-shih</u>, 308.10a-17b; and that by K.W. So in <u>Draft Ming Biographies</u>, no. 9 (1968).

21. Hsia Hsieh, chüan 60 (vol. 3, p. 2327).

22. See the biographies of Yüan O and Yü Ta-yu in Ming-shih, 205.13b-14a and 212.1a-8b. Also see Yüan O's letter to Hu Tsung-hsien during the siege of T'ung-hsiang, reproduced in Ts'ai Chiu-te's Wo-pien shih-lüeh (Chung-kuo li-shih yen-chiu tzu-liao ts'ung-shu ed.; reprint, volume 15, pp. 69-117), pp. 101-102. Yü Ta-yu, an excellent subject for a biographical study, had a record of successful "pacification" of rebellious southwestern aborigines prior to serving in Chekiang and in 1555 cautiously advised Supreme Commander Chang Ching against attacking marauders too hastily. But in 1557 he vigorously opposed proposals to appease Wang Chih with trading opportunities.

23. The basic sources on Wang Chih and the campaign against him are those mentioned in note 18 above, especially Wang Chih chuan and Fu Wei-lin, chüan 162, pp. 3213-3217. Also see the biography of Hu Tsung-hsien in Ming-shih, 205.8a-14a; and Ryūsaku Tsunoda, translator, Japan in the Chinese Dynastic Histories: Later Han through Ming Dynasties (ed. by L. Carrington Goodrich; South Pasadena, 1951), pp. 128-137.

24. For the general nature of the Ming military establishment, see C. O. Hucker, "Governmental Organization of the Ming Dynasty," pp. 56-63; Romeyn Taylor's "Yüan Origins of the Wei-so System" in Chinese Government in Ming Times: Seven Studies (ed. by C. O. Hucker; New York, 1969), pp. 23-40; and James F. Millinger, pp. 14-19.

25. For military organization in Chekiang in the 1550's see James F. Millinger, pp. 26-40; Ch'ou-hai t'u-pien, 5.8a-17b; and Fan Lai's Liang-Che hai-fang lei-k'ao hsü-pien, chüan 2.

26. Ch'ou-hai t'u-pien, 5.11a-17b.

27. See Li Kuang-ming's special study of this practice, cited in note 1 above.

28. Ch'ou-hai t'u-pien, 5.11a-17b.

29. Mao K'un, Chi chiao Hsü Hai pen-mo (Mao Lu-men hsien-sheng wen-chi, Wan-li ed., 30.20a-30b), 30.20a-b. For Tsung Li, see his brief biography in Ming-shih, 205.9b.

30. See the biographies of Kuei Yu-kuang and T'ang Shun-chih in

Ming-shih, 287. 20b-21b, 205. 20b-22b. Also see Wu Yü-nien for Ming writings on Wako activities in the Southeast.

31. See note 1 above.

32. See the biography of Mao K'un in Ming-shih, 287.12b-13a. His chronicle of the campaign against Hsü Hai is known generally by the title Hsü Hai pen-mo. The text primarily cited in this article, titled Chi chiao Hsü Hai pen-mo, appears in the Wan-li edition of Mao's collected works, Mao Lu-men hsien-sheng wen-chi, 30. 20a-30b. Other early texts occur in Ch'ou-hai t'u-pien, 9. 12a-19a; and Chekiang t'ung-chih (attributed to the sponsorship of Hu Tsung-hsien; preface dated 1561), 60. 21b-25a. The work has been republished in such collectanea as Chieh-yüeh shan-fang hui-ch'ao, Tse-ku-chai ch'ung-ch'ao, and Chung-kuo li-shih yen-chiu tzu-liao ts'ung-shu. See bibliographic discussions in Wu Yü-nien, p. 242; and in Wolfgang Franke, p. 223.

33. Ts'ai Chiu-te is sometimes referred to as Sung 宋 Chiu-te or as Chu 朱 Chiu-te. His chronicle, reportedly based on government files, is known as Wo-pien shih-lüeh. The text cited in this article appears in Chung-kuo li-shih yen-chiu tzu-liao ts'ung-shu, volume 15, pp. 69-117. It also appears in such collectanea as Yen-i chih-lin, Sheng-ch'ao i-shih, and Ts'ung-shu chi-ch'eng ch'u-pien. See biblio-graphic discussions in Wu Yü-nien, pp. 235-236; and in Wolfgang Franke, p. 223.

34. The 1940 photolithographic reprint is the edition of Shih-tsung shih-lu cited in this article. Other materials relied upon include the biography of Hu Tsung-hsien in Ming-shih, 205. 8a-14a; Hsia Hsieh's Ming t'ung-chien; Ku Ying-t'ai's Ming-shih chi-shih pen-mo, chüan 55; and Wang Chih chuan.

35. Mao K'un (30. 20b) suggests that Hu personally took up a defensive position at the Grand Canal town T'ang-ch'i near Chia-hsing.

36. Ts'ai Chiu-te, pp. 98-99.

37. Shih-tsung shih-lu, 434. 7a.

38. Mao K'un, 30. 22a.

39. Mao K'un, 30.24a. The text indicates that troops were ordered from Chia-hsing to Tou-men 斗門. Tou-men is a common place name. There are several places in Chekiang so named, but I have not yet identified the place that is meant here.

40. Ts'ai Chiu-te, pp. 101-102. Cf. Wu Ch'ung-han, p. 69.

41. Mao K'un, 30.22b.

42. Shih-tsung shih-lu, 435.5b.

43. Shih-tsung shih-lu, 435.3a-b; Ku Ying-t'ai, chüan 55 (section 8, p. 53).

44. Ts'ai Chiu-te, p. 102.

45. Mao K'un reports that Hsü Hai and Ch'en Tung withdrew separately from T'ung-hsiang but gives no details about their routes of withdrawal. Ts'ai Chiu-te (pp. 102-103) is followed here, although his report is not wholly clear.

46. Ts'ai Chiu-te, p. 102; Ku Ying-t'ai, chüan 55 (section 8, p. 54).

47. See Fu Wei-lin, 162.3216; Wang Chih chuan (unpaged).

48. Shih-tsung shih-lu, 437.1a-b; Hsia Hsieh, chüan 61 (vol. 3, pp. 2358-2359).

49. Ts'ai Chiu-te, p. 102.

50. Shih-tsung shih-lu, 436.2b.

51. Mao K'un, 30.25a-b. Ts'ai Chiu-te reports that the marauders comprised three distinct groups: one led by Hsü Hai, one led by Hung Tung-kang 洪東岡 and others, and a third led by Ch'en Tung, Yeh Ma, and others (pp. 102-103). Ts'ai also gives the impression that Hsü Hai arranged for this Hung Tung-kang to be taken into custody (p. 105), not supporting Mao K'un's report that the "Hung" in question was Hsü Hai's younger brother, thus Hsü Hung. I find no support for Ts'ai's version of this incident in other sources, and no references elsewhere to anyone named Hung Tung-kang.

52. Shih-tsung shih-lu, 436.3a.

53. Ts'ai Chiu-te, pp. 104-105; Mao K'un, 30.25b.

54. Mao K'un, 30.26b.

55. Mao K'un, 30.27a. Ts'ai Chiu-te suggests that the idea of baiting the marauders with boats may have originated with Hsü Hai himself (p.104).

56. Mao K'un, 30.27a.

57. Mao K'un, 30.27a-b; Ts'ai Chiu-te, p. 107; Shih-tsung shih-lu, 437.3b-4a.

58. Mao K'un, 30.27b-28a. Cf. Ku Ying-t'ai, chüan 55 (section 8, p.54).

59. Ts'ai Chiu-te, pp. 107-108.

60. Mao K'un, 30.28a.

61. I have not been able to determine the precise location of the estate called Shen-chia-chuang or, sometimes, Shen-chuang. The sources make it clear that the estate could not have been far from P'ing-hu city.

62. Ts'ai Chiu-te, p. 108.

63. Ku Ying-t'ai, chüan 55 (section 8, p. 54).

64. Ts'ai Chiu-te, pp. 108-109.

65. Mao K'un, 30.29a.

66. Mao K'un, 30.29b; Ts'ai Chiu-te, pp. 109-112; Ku Ying-t'ai, chüan 55 (section 8, p. 54).

67. Shih-tsung shih-lu, 439.5b-6a,6b-7a.

68. Ming-shih, 205.10b.

69. See the biography of Hu Tsung-hsien in <u>Ming-shih</u>, 205.8a–14a.

70. <u>Ming-shih</u>, 205.23a.

71. Cited in Wu Ch'ung-han, p. 88.

72. C.O. Hucker, ed., <u>Chinese Government in Ming Times: Seven Studies</u>, p. 72.

73. Mao K'un, 30.20b.

74. Ts'ai Chiu-te, p. 99.

# SU-CHOU AND THE AGENTS OF WEI CHUNG-HSIEN, 1626

## INTRODUCTION

K'ai-tu ch'uan-hsin 開讀傳信 is a narrative account of a popular uprising that occurred in the Chinese city of Su-chou in the spring of 1626 on the occasion of the promulgation of an order for the arrest of the scholar-official Chou Shun-ch'ang 周順昌 (1584-1626). This was not one of the numerous "peasant rebellions" that marked the final fifteen years of Ming rule and that are now attracting attention among the mainland Chinese. It was, rather, a spontaneous demonstration, by literati and commoners alike and in one of the wealthiest and most populous metropolitan centers of Ming China, in defense of a member of the official class who had been doomed to die because of his obstinate adherence to Confucian morality, and in defiance of a ruthless and heterodox clique that had usurped imperial authority and disrupted the processes and principles of traditional Confucian politics.

In 1626 Chinese political morality was at one of its lowest ebbs. On the throne at Peking was an incompetent 21-year-old Emperor, known to history primarily by his temple name Hsi Tsung (reigned 1620-1627).[1] Much too occupied with puttering at carpentry to pay attention to the government, he had gladly permitted his governess, one Madame K'o 客氏 (d. ca. 1627), to install her favorite, the illiterate and unscrupulous eunuch Wei Chung-hsien 魏忠賢 (1568-1627),[2] in posts of the greatest trust and responsibility within the palace; and Wei, through the most brutal terrorism, had made himself undisputed master of the imperial household and the sole instrument through which imperial authority was transmitted to the vast bureaucratic mechanism that administered China.

Within the bureaucracy itself an intense partisan struggle had been in progress for more than twenty years. On one side was a large group of men known to their friends as "advocates of righteousness" (ch'ing-i) and at least to their enemies as the Eastern Forest Party (Tung-lin tang) because of their connections with an Eastern Forest Academy (Tung-lin

41

shu-yüan), who on the whole stood for integrity and justice in government. Opposing them, a consortium of partisan cliques had attached
itself to a succession of Grand Secretariat ministers and opportunist-
ically practised a sort of government by crony.[3] In 1621, after the
death of the antagonistic Emperor Shen Tsung (reigned 1572-1620),[4]
the "advocates of righteousness" had gained control of the most important
high-level government offices. But their outspoken attacks on the
rising Wei Chung-hsien and the machinations of their dispossessed or
about-to-be-dispossessed enemies had given the so-called "traitor
eunuch" cause and opportunity to extend his influence from the palace
into the civil administration. The long partisan struggle thereupon
reached an undreamed-of climax in 1625 and 1626 when "advocates of
righteousness" were systematically dismissed, "erased from the rolls"
and thus deprived of their official status and prerogatives, and in some
instances cruelly put to death.

The arrest of Chou Shun-ch'ang in the spring of 1626 was one of a
long series of injustices committed by Wei Chung-hsien and his henchmen. Chou[5] was a native of Wu, one of three districts with headquarters
in the city of Su-chou, the center of Su-chou prefecture. Su-chou in
turn was an acknowledged center of the rich and influential area around
modern Shanghai known as "the southeast" or as Chiang-nan, whose
literati were the core of the "advocates of righteousness" and suffered
most under Wei's purges. Chou won his doctoral degree (chin-shih) in
1613, served until 1619 in prefectural duties in Fukien province, and
then held a succession of posts in the Ministry of Civil Service at the
capital, becoming in the end vice-director (yüan-wai-lang) of the
Ministry's Department of Civil Selections. A stickler for honesty, he
tried to inject his own austere and incorruptible spirit into the process
by which official appointments were distributed.[6] It has been said
that he hated evil as a personal enemy;[7] and, though he perhaps could
not originally have been considered an active member of the Eastern
Forest Party, he did find that his views were congenial with those of
the active Eastern Forest partisans with whom he came in contact.[8]
In 1622, before the rise of Wei Chung-hsien to complete power, Chou
returned to his home on extended leave of absence. It was while living
at home, as the following text relates, that he became overtly critical
of the eunuch and his clique, with the result that his arrest was ordered.
Despite the disturbance that attended this event, Chou in the end was
taken under custody to the capital, imprisoned, tortured, and secretly
put to death.

* * *

The narrative that is translated in full in the following pages, K'ai-tu ch'uan-hsin or The True Story of the Promulgation, is the most comprehensive extant account of the incident at Su-chou. It appears in Sung-t'ien lu-pi (chüan 22, pp. 1a-14b, among addenda), a source book on the anti-Wei Chung-hsien struggle that was edited by the Su-chou commoner Chin Jih-sheng 金日升 (fl. in the 1620's and 1630's) and published in 24 chüan in the Ch'ung-chen period (1628-1644); the preface is dated 1629. An identical text, but lacking the postface that is appended to the Sung-t'ien lu-pi text (14b-15a), occurs in the old manuscript collection Pi-ts'e ts'ung-shuo 秘册叢説 (volume 13, pp. 15a-27a), which may have been compiled before the fall of the Ming dynasty in 1644.[9] A third version, also lacking the postface and otherwise greatly abridged, occurs in Ssŭ-ch'ao ta-cheng lu (2.28a-34b), an account of late Ming partisan struggles that was compiled by Liu Hsin-hsüeh 劉心學 (1599-1674) and published in two chüan in 1831. The translation given here is of the Sung-t'ien lu-pi text but does not include the postface.

Identity of the author of K'ai-tu ch'uan-hsin has not been generally agreed upon, but there appears to be a strong probability that it is the work of Wen Chen-heng 文震亨 (1585-1645), a resident of Su-chou, a friend of Chou Shun-ch'ang, and, as eyewitnesses testify, an active participant in the uprising described. This being the case, this text's lengthy discussion between Wen Chen-heng himself and the authorities in charge of the promulgation ceremony, which in any case would be suspect because of its unsupported glorification of Wen, can hardly be considered credible.[10] Nevertheless, that K'ai-tu ch'uan-hsin is in other regards a reasonably reliable account of the Su-chou uprising and the events that immediately preceded and followed it is substantiated by comparison with other sources relevant to the incident. Among these are accounts by proved eyewitnesses such as Yin Hsien-ch'en 殷獻 臣 (d. 1645),[11] Chu Tsu-wen 朱祖文 (d. 1626),[12] and Yang T'ing-shu 楊 廷樞 (1595-1647);[13] accounts by contemporary Su-chou residents such as the aforementioned Chin Jih-sheng,[14] Chang Shih-wei 張世偉 (1568-1641),[15] (who might have been eyewitnesses,) and Yao Hsi-meng 姚希孟 (1579-1636);[16] a contemporary account by an author identified only as "the wave minister of the five lakes" (五湖波臣 ) that quite possibly is an eyewitness account;[17] and official reports submitted to the capital by the authorities concerned, themselves eyewitnesses.[18]

These and other materials have been drawn upon freely to authenticate, broaden, or clarify the following K'ai-tu ch'uan-hsin narrative in notes or, in cases of interesting variations of detail, in parenthetical insertions into the body of the translation.

\* \* \*

## K'AI-TU CH'UAN-HSIN*

At the time of the arrest of Wei Ta-chung 魏大中 (1575-1625),[19] the former Ministry of Civil Service departmental vice-director Chou Shun-ch'ang was living at home in Wu-men (i. e., Su-chou). Shun-ch'ang had long enjoyed a great reputation for purity and resoluteness, and his whole life had been devoted to loyalty and patriotism. When Ta-chung passed through Wu, Shun-chang treated him cordially and through successive days was constantly in his company. In parting, he wept bitterly and betrothed his daughter to (Wei's) grandson; and when mention was made of the new influence of the inner court (i.e., the palace eunuchs), he viciously gnashed his teeth and vigorously cursed, while everyone stared.

As always when the traitor-eunuch (Wei Chung-hsien) sent out guardsmen (t'i-ch'i 緹騎, i.e., members of the Imperial Guard, Chin-i wei), men had been sent along behind to spy in their wake. They saw Shun-ch'ang grasping hands and being affectionate with Ta-chung. And when, because the delay had become so extended, the guardsmen urged Ta-chung along and spoke disrespectfully to Shun-ch'ang, Shun-ch'ang in wide-eyed indignation abused them, saying: "Don't you know there are men in the world who aren't afraid to die? You go back and tell Chung-hsien that I am the former Ministry of Civil Service departmental vice-director Chou Shun-ch'ang!" Then he called out the name of Chung-hsien and cursed it ceaselessly. Observers gaped at one another and put out their tongues in astonishment, and his words were reported to Chung-hsien.

Later (Wei) Ta-chung was sent to prison. The censor Ni Wen-huan 倪文煥 (chin-shih 1619) then impeached Shun-ch'ang because of the marriage agreement, and he was erased from the rolls (i.e., deprived of his status and prerogatives as an official).[20]

[The "wave minister of the five lakes" reports: "It had happened

*The translator gladly acknowledges indebtedness to his friends Mr. Chao Pao-ch'u and Professor Hiraoka Takeo for many suggestions that enhanced his understanding of this text; but he accepts full responsibility for the translation offered.

that the vice-prefect Yang Chiang 楊姜 ,[21] because he obstinately refused to cooperate with the eunuch supervisor of textile manufactures, Li Shih 李實 (ca. 1570-ca. 1636),[22] was falsely memorialized about and dismissed from office. Tradition was that eunuchs did not impeach functionaries of prefectures and districts or encroach upon the authority of governors and provincial inspectors. But when (Chou 周) Ch'i-yüan 起元 (1572-1626),[23] who was governor, attempted to defend (Yang), Ch'i-yüan himself was also dismissed. On the day when he departed from Wu, Shun-ch'ang as a parting gift to him wrote an essay of several hundred words dripping with lamentations, in which he made critical references (to Wei Chung-hsien) without the slightest concealment.[24] Thus he, too, aroused the hatred of Chung-hsien. Instructions were given to the new governor, Mao I-lu 毛一鷺 (chin-shih 1604),[25] secretly to spy around. Shun-ch'ang put an end to all his interventions and pleadings; he remained in solitude and took no part in affairs. His house of a few rafters in a winding lane merely sheltered his body from wind and rain, and he ate poor-quality rice. His wife, Madame Wu 吳氏, had never been accustomed to gold or pearls; she only possessed one or two silver hairpins, and for the better part of a year they had been in a pawnshop. Therefore, no flaw could ever be found in him. The (Wei Chung-hsien) partisan Ni Wen-huan was urged to impeach him. Having no evidence, he made inquiries of (Chou's) fellow-townsman So-and-so. This So-and-so, who had been disposed of in the merit evaluations but remained in the capital, had once been reproved by Shun-ch'ang. Thinking of revenge, he fabricated evidence and offered it; and then Shun-ch'ang was erased from the rolls. " (T'i-ch'i chi-lüeh, pp. 26b-27a.) ]

Chung-hsien's hatred was not yet exhausted. Before this, the censor serving as provincial inspector at Wu [i. e. , Hsü Chi 徐吉 (chin-shih 1616) ] and the censor-in-chief (chung-ch'eng) serving as governor of Wu, Mao I-lu, both held grudges against Shun-ch'ang because of breaches in courtesy. And when the former governor Chou Ch'i-yüan impeached a censorial superviser of military defenses[26] for requesting leave of absence on a false pretext of illness and it was ordered that Ch'i-yüan himself be erased from the rolls, they then said the memorial had actually been written by Shun-ch'ang. Thereupon the eunuch superviser of textile manufactures, Li Shih, retroactively accused Ch'i-yüan of having reduced, on his own authority, the originally-prescribed quota of cloth for imperial gowns and of having obstructed transportation. Moreover, he said that, under the pretext of studying the Tao, he had gathered associates and friends about him in a partisan faction; that Chou Tsung-chien周宗建 (1582-1626),[27] Miao Ch'ang-ch'i.繆昌期 (1562-1626),[28] Chou Shun-ch'ang, Kao P'an-lung高攀龍 (1562-1626),[29] Li Ying-sheng李應昇 (1593-1626),[30] and Huang Tsun-su黃尊素 (1584-1626),[31] sought favors from him; and the people of Wu were gnashing their teeth in profound anger.[32]

Even before, because of a memorial by the Shansi governor, K'o Ch'ang 柯昶 (chin-shih 1604), regarding the banishment of Chang Shen-yen張慎言 (1568-1646) to frontier military service, Chung-hsien had already said in a forged rescript: "Chou Tsung-chien's bribery plunder is wantonly excessive. The governor and the provincial inspector were to conduct an investigation, but after a long time there has been no memorial in reply and, moreover, he is allowed to roam about at leisure without a care. And Miao Ch'ang-ch'i, though already erased from the rolls and stripped of his honors, still wears official robes, carries yellow parasols, and accumulates hangers-on in his private residence. Let guardsmen arrest them both for trial."[33]

When (Li) Shih's memorial was submitted, Chung-hsien made further plots. Ts'ui Ch'eng-hsiu崔呈秀 (chin-shih 1613, d. 1627)[34] and others said: "If they are not all arrested, authority cannot be established." Thereupon he further ordered the arrest of Ch'i-yüan and the others, five men in all.[35]

As regards the memorial submitted by (Li) Shih: When he arrived at Wu from Che (-chiang), it was rumored, the censor-in-chief set forth a feast to entertain him, with several hundred kinds of sea and land delicacies. Shih never once touched them with his chopsticks and the censor-in-chief was quite abashed. Only when, at last, he took one sip of tea did the censor-in-chief, relieved, bring up the matter of Shun-ch'ang. Moreover, he implicated two or three other officials from Wu, wishing to trap all in one net. But Shih had heard only of Chung-hsien's hatred for Shun-ch'ang and therefore dared not involve others.

(On the other hand,) some say that the memorial was prepared in Shih's name in the inner court, that neither Shih nor the censor-in-chief had any part in it, and that the matter was so secret that no one knew of it.[36]

During this period guardsmen, relying upon (public dread of) Chung-hsien, all became abusive and arrogant. Wherever they went prefects and magistrates prepared official residences and food for them; and lesser local officials who in the slightest regard did not meet with their approval were forthwith given official beatings. (The guardsmen) even treated governors as equals without engaging in courtesies, and governors behaved toward them with deference. From the families of the victims of their arrests they demanded money by the thousands (of taels), utterly ruining them.

(Miao) Ch'ang-ch'i and (Chou) Tsung-chien had not been gone three days when other guardsmen arrived in Wu to arrest Shun-ch'ang.[37] The hubbub in Wu reached a climax.

[Chang Shih-wei reports: "In their hearts everyone knew that (the arrest of Chou Tsung-chien) was the doing of the traitor Wei, that in court he had ordered the arrest and trial. Everyone was very agitated. Subsequently there was not a day when they did not alarm one another about arrests by the guardsmen. They would say: 'On such a day at such a time they will come again!' They also said: ' On such a day they will come to arrest So-and-so!' In general, all those 'So-and-so's' whose arrests were rumored were men who were currently renowned for loyalty but had been erased from the rolls. Moreover, it was thought: 'The traitor Wei is going to do as he likes, and with his various villains he plots to kill off all those in the empire who do not toady to him so that afterwards he might monopolize power.' They talked with a great clamor and pointed to the vice censor-in-chief Chou (Tsung-chien) as evidence. They also said: 'When the vice censor-in-chief reached such-and-such a place, he was put to death with poison, and his corpse was abandoned in such-and-such a place. In short, when there is a forged edict there is no waiting for imprisonment and trial.' Many people believed all this." (Chou Li-pu chi-shih, pp. 8b-9a.)]

Shun-ch'ang, while living at home, enjoyed going before the governmental authorities on behalf of the common people to cry out for justice and to restrain oppression; in all lightening of corvée requirements or delaying of tax collections, it always was Shun-ch'ang who was in the forefront. He associated intimately with poor scholars, praising and recommending them unstintingly. Consequently, literati and common-ers alike were profoundly convinced of his virtue; and when suddenly they learned of the disaster that had come upon him, they were over-come with outraged anger and wanted to take his place. There was a great clamor, and everyone blamed the censor-in-chief.

When the news arrived, the day became dark as night; there were wild winds and furious rains. For five days and nights in succession rain poured down. On level ground water became several feet deep!

Shun-ch'ang lived on a winding lane outside the city wall, in desolate surroundings behind a poor wicker gate. When the order (for his arrest) arrived at Wu, the district magistrate Ch'en Wen-jui 陳文瑞 (chin-shih 1625), who had long and highly esteemed Shun-ch'ang, [38] dismissed his attendants and, braving the rain, went in the night to tell him about it. Shun-ch'ang's countenance did not change. They sat and chatted for a long time, and then the magistrate asked Shun-ch'ang to go in and prepare his baggage.

[Chang Shih-wei reports: "(When the magistrate arrived,) Li-pu ("the Ministry of Civil Service," i.e., Chou Shun-ch'ang) said with spirit: 'I have been prepared for arrest for a long time! But I regret that because I have been erased from the rolls I am unable to appeal and in the presence of the Emperor unfold what I would like to say. If a prisoner might memorialize, I might be able to denounce those in power so that the various villains might know that loyal men in the world cannot all be murdered. Then even death might be assuaged in one's glorification.'" (Chou Li-pu chi-shih, pp. 9a-9b.)]

Shun-ch'ang since leaving office had liked to study calligraphy, and he was so fond of inscribing things for others that he never tired. When he went in and looked over his documents, he moistened a pen and wrote an inscription for a monk. [39] His wife and children all wept in a circle before him, but Shun-ch'ang was unmoved and in his conversation never alluded to any personal matter.

At dawn Shun-ch'ang watched the magistrate consume two bowls of congee. Only then did he change into prisoner's garb. Sedan-chair bearers were called, and he got in. The road was blocked by those who watched, and all wept until they lost their voices.

When he had entered the yamen to await orders, from the governor's palace near the yamen the censor-in-chief secretly sent a man to spy around. He saw that the common people, young and old alike, were arriving in swarms, all wishing to get a glimpse of Chou Li-pu (i.e., "Chou of the Ministry of Civil Service"). Some cursed, and some prayed. Those who cursed called the censor-in-chief a traitor-partisan. Students[40] in their (formal-dress) green collars ran about in the mud and mire. From dawn till midday and on into afternoon the streets were solidly filled.

The censor-in-chief, fearful, instructed the district magistrate to ask Shun-ch'ang to another yamen in the district for drink, food, and bathing. The literati and commoners all followed. The yamen being too small to admit them, they all became rain-soaked in the courtyard; but talk about their leaving was not to be endured.

["The wave minister of the five lakes" reports: "The governor, estimating that popular feelings could not be restrained, ordered the local authorities repeatedly to move Shun-ch'ang about. In one day he was moved four or five times. Far and near there was increased agitation, so that the alleys were choked and the roads blocked. Carriers of burdens rested their shoulders, and shopkeepers closed their businesses. In tens and hundreds they formed into groups, running about to make inquiries, or weeping, or angrily cursing, or smiting their foreheads and imploring heaven, or paying for divination to determine good and evil omens. White-haired elders, weeping, said to one another: 'Why should the court put a good man to death?' Others replied: 'What has this to do with the court? Of course, it is merely that the eunuch Wei wants to kill him.' Some said: 'We are mean fellows. Why do we shrink so from our own deaths that we do not beg for the life of Li-pu?' Some prepared grief-filled pleas and submitted them to the authorities. Some wished hurriedly to pack and go to the capital to ask for justice. There were those who, though not familiar with Li-pu's face, on getting one look at him knocked their heads as if gazing upon some auspicious omen. Those who crowded around blocking the way so that no one could go forward called out his name from outside the gate and repeatedly paid him homage. All sighed and sobbed; tears flowed freely. They could not bear to leave: they went out by (early morning) starlight and returned home (at night) by starlight. From the fifteenth day to the eighteenth day (i.e., from April 11 to April 14, 1626) the whole region was as disrupted as if (everyone) were rushing to the assistance of distressed parents." (T'i-ch'i chi-lüeh, pp. 27b-28b.]

[Chang Shih-wei reports: "At first Li-pu was lodged in the district yamen. The crowd followed him to the district yamen and every day stood there talking by the thousands and hundreds. They talked about loyalty in ancient and modern times and urged on laggards not to mind appearances. Those who emerged from interviews said that Li-pu not only had overcome fear but also was not bitterly wrathful; that, merely because of his breast's being full of pure sincerity, he shone like a flash of lightning or fire struck from a flint. Nevertheless, he denounced the eunuch increasingly." (Chou Li-pu chi-shih, p. 9b.]

Shun-ch'ang's family was bitterly poor and lacked even a single picul of stored supplies; yet the guardsmen intimidated it ceaselessly. Shun-ch'ang, however, swore that he would not give them a single coin. Thereupon the literati and commoners all wished to pour out their possessions in his aid. Even those who ordinarily lacked good principles begrudged nothing, and there even were some who left money and departed without mentioning their names. Poor scholars borrowed against their tutorial salaries and, that being thought insufficient, handed over their poor clothes to pawnshops, and the little that they obtained they forthwith presented as gifts. The guardsmen, learning of this, ever-increasingly yearned to fill up their purses. Only after lingering for three days did they issue their summons.

On this day it again rained heavily. After the crowd had heard the summons, Shun-ch'ang was put into a caged cart. The whole city went along, everyone escorting him carrying incense. Smoke billowed up to obscure heaven, and the sound of the crying out for justice reverberated for several tens of miles (li). As the district magistrate accompanied Shun-ch'ang out of the district yamen, the crowd blocked the way so

that the cart could not go forward. Shun-ch'ang lifted up its screen
and persuasively said: "I am deeply moved that my fathers and brothers
covet me and wish to retain me a little while. But it is the law of the
state! It cannot be delayed for a moment! My fathers and brothers, let
us here say goodbye!" At this, the crowd grieved even more. From
the district yamen to the guardsmen's compound[41] was a distance of
not one mile (li), but every few steps the crowd hindered them so that
they could not proceed, and only after a long while did they get through.

["The wave minister of the five lakes" reports: "Those
among the students who knew him made plans with one another,
saying: 'The people are indeed angry. What will happen when
(the edict) is opened and read cannot be foretold. Let us, on
his behalf, request that grief not be inflicted on the whole area.
Then, together with two or three elders, they went everywhere
consoling the common people, saying: 'The court and the
sagely-wise ruler all consider Li-pu to be loyal and patriotic
and wish that he live. If we wish to plan for Li-pu's safety,
we must instantly beg for his life before the two dignitaries
(i. e. , the censor-in-chief / governor and the censor / provincial
inspector,) but being careful not to go to excess and cause
trouble.' The common people all said: 'Agreed!' Thereupon
all went carrying incense from Wu district to the guardsmen's
compound. Those who accompanied Shun-ch'ang were several
tens of thousands. Their weeping and wailing shook heaven,
and their wiping away of tears formed rain. The horses of the
district officials were unable to go forward. The day had
reached noon; lowering clouds were black and ugly, mixed
with flying frost. There was not a man whose heart and
spirit were not agitated and downcast. " (T'i-ch'i chi-lüeh,
p. 28b.)]

After arriving at the guardsmen's compound, the crowd increased.
The gates not yet having been opened, and the compound being close
against the city wall, a crowd climbed atop the wall and stood round on
the parapets, which all became filled. Incense burned in the rain like
an array of torches. When men atop the wall called out, men below the
wall answered; and when men below the wall called out, then men atop
the wall similarly answered. The noise became increasingly thunderous.
Shun-ch'ang himself was taken by surprise and with the utmost respect
requested that they disperse. But the crowd did not make a move.

Meantime, teachers and elders had all assembled, and some proposed going to the capital to submit memorials demanding justice for Shun-ch'ang.

The battalion commanders and the guardsmen of the Imperial Guard,[42] inside the compound, were all terrified and wished to urge the censor-in-chief to enter and augment their strength. Meanwhile the superviser of defenses Chang Hsiao 張孝 , the prefect K'ou Shen 寇慎 (chin-shih 1616), and the magistrate (Ch'en) Wen-jui, all of whom in their hearts recognized the injustice being done Shun-ch'ang, looked at one another with grieved countenances. The panic in the people's minds had previously been reported to the provincial inspector, Hsü Chi. When the censor (i.e., Hsü Chi) arrived, his front-runners shouted to clear the way as in ordinary times. But when the censor saw the scene he was shocked and warned them not to clear the people away. As soon as the censor-in-chief arrived, the crowd thrice cried out "An unequalled injustice!" They all repeatedly echoed it.

To the left of the compound gate had been placed seats for the two dignitaries. Some students were going to wait until (the dignitaries) entered and sat down facing the prefect and the magistrate; then they wished to make a request that they prostrate themselves before the throne and submit memorials. But the censor-in-chief wished abruptly to terminate the affair. As soon as he arrived he ordered the gates opened, and literati and commoners promptly swarmed inside.

Now the rain lessened and stopped, but the ground was a mire of mud, knee-deep. The students entirely disregarded it. Having entered, they gazed up at the screens and insignia set up on the platform. The two Imperial Guard officers stood like sentinels in their black uniforms, gazing in all directions as haughtily as if no one were near. Below them had been set up some manacling instruments, and there the victim of arrest lay prostrate. The students were increasingly overcome with indignation. Some gazed up toward heaven and issued long wails, and others called upon T'ai Tsu Kao Huang Ti (the eunuch-hating founder of the Ming dynasty). Their words were a jumble that could not be distinguished. But there still was none who spoke out firmly to state their complaint.

When the two dignitaries came inside, one student, Wen Chen-heng, greeted them and said: "Today, when the feelings of the people and the

minds of the literati are such as this, can you honorable gentlemen alone
not keep the historians in mind so as to glorify yourselves?" The
censor-in-chief knit his brows and said: "I always think of such things,
but today what can be done?" The student said: "This is the plan for
today: We request that the opening and reading (of the edict) be delayed
and that you honorable gentlemen report the true facts to the Emperor,
stating that the literati and people urgently cry out for no other reason
than that they wish to pray for the vast and magnificent imperial mercy
in order that Li-pu might be turned over to the governor and the provincial inspector for investigation. If there is evidence that he has
sought favors, then let him be arrested and put to death forthwith, and
there will be no remorse."

The censor-in-chief had absolutely no intention of permitting this,
but because the statement was just, he feigned a cordial manner and
said: "To submit memorials on behalf of Li-pu would indeed be proper.
But you students have not yet given this thorough consideration. The
imperial anger being so great, if memorials are submitted, can they
guarantee that he will be aided?" The student said: "Certainly, if it
were a question of the imperial anger, then how could it be shirked?
But nowadays edicts are actually forged by Chung-hsien, so that he
might murder worthy literati and officials of the empire to satisfy his
own personal anger. Chung-hsien's poison flows not only to one region,
and disaster is suffered not only by one man! Li-pu, especially, is one
to whom we students have long submitted our hearts. And when we
actually see that it is merely because of talk (not actual deeds) that he
has come to disaster, we do not shrink from the axes and choppers in
begging for his life. If now a memorial is submitted, and if you honorable gentlemen will kindly tell the whole story, we may be fortunate
enough to obtain what we request; and then the time of Li-pu's re-birth
will be a time when (the memory of) you honorable gentlemen will
become imperishable. And even if we do not obtain what we request,
even so, your moral uprightness will be preserved in men's minds
deathlessly. Can you honorable gentlemen not hold back even this
single advocate of righteousness so as to humble the scoundrel's gall
and make him know what he must shrink from?"

The censor-in-chief had no response to offer. He only said: "You
students all study and emulate Confucius. Have you not heard that in
the ruler-subject relationship there is actually no place of escape? Now
the edict is here; that is, the ruler-father is here! How can gathering

in crowds and raising a clamor be the proper conduct of subjects?'
The student said: "How can it be merely (a question of) an imperial
edict's being here? Take the imperial ancestors as a practical model!
When Chung-hsien's forgeries and usurpations can be seen to have
reached this extreme, he should immediately be put to death! In former days we students certainly served the honorable gentleman with
respect; and if by obeying your instructions we should win insignificant
places on the jade staircase (before the throne), we would certainly
remonstrate unto death about affairs such as to day's. How could re-
sisting the imperial wrath be the responsibility of other men? How
could the honorable gentleman teach men to cringe and toady? We
have only listened in the streets and do not entirely know how this
affair originated. Therefore we wish that the honorable gentleman
manage it. This activity today is for your sake, sir, not Li-pu's!"

All this while the censor bent his ear to listen. Noting the
ardor of the student's words, he officiously said: "Don't you students
clamor so; we must deliberate about bringing affairs to a good end. "
The censor-in-chief said: "Accordingly, let (the edict) be opened and
read!"

The student said: "Honorable sir, your words are mere mock-
ery. After the opening and reading, it can only be that he will instantly depart; and if he departs, it can only be that he will instantly
die. What can be done than?"

Now the guardsmen looked at one another and whispered: "Who
is this?" They were amazed that the censor-in-chief did not take
punitive action against the student. The student then said to the
censor-in-chief: "We students today have already risked the more.
If you honorable gentlemen sacrifice your offices, and if we students
sacrifice our lives, then there may be unexpected results. Have you
honorable gentlemen not heard of past affairs in Wu? When (the
great eunuch) Wang Chih (fl. in the 1480's) was in power, he sent the
eunuch Wang Ching 王敬 by courier service to Wu, and the students
were ordered to copy out unorthodox books. The students did not
obey. Ching ordered the local authorities to arrest them and bring them
to the courier station, wishing to humiliate them; but the students
picked up clubs, sought him out, and attacked him in the street. Ching
fled into hiding, barely escaping with his life. The minister (of war)
Wang Shu 王恕 (1416-1508), who was then governor of Chiang-nan, memorialized and laid the blame on Ching. Ching was punished, and the students escaped.[43] I have also heard that when (the eunuch) Wang Chen 王振

(d. 1449) was in power, he hated the National Academy chancellor Li Shih-mien 李時勉 (ca. 1374-1450) because of his obstinate rectitude and ordered him put in a cangue at the gate of the National Academy. Several thousand National Academy students went to the palace to get Chen and have revenge on him. Chen became terrified, and Shih-mien obtained his release.[44] Now these men have let loose a tiger and have given it wings (i. e. , have made it even more dangerous), and have aroused the anger of the mob to be like (uncontrollable) water and fire. What can they rely on so as to be unafraid? It is merely for the sake of you honorable gentlemen that they are protected. "

On hearing this the guardsmen all shrank back. But the censor-in-chief spoke on, saying: "If you wish a memorial to be submitted, you must wait until I enter my palace and prepare a draft. " The student said: "Once the honorable gentleman has entered his palace would we students be permitted to see his face again? It is necessary to prepare the memorial here; that will do. "

The censor then turned to the censor-in-chief and said with spirit: "(The great remonstrators of antiquity Kuan 關) Lung-p'ang 龍逄 [45] and Pi Kan 比干, [46] after all, were only men. Today we two ought to exert ourselves! " And the superviser of defenses from the side also vigorously urged them on. Now there was a thread of hope in the affair!

All the while the two dignitaries and the student were talking together, back and forth, the crowd encircled them like a wall, listening. The two dignitaries were standing upright in the mud; their shoulders jarred together, and they could not even stand steadily on the ground. They no longer had any dignity of demeanor! There was such a great clamor that the crowd could not make out what the student and the dignitaries were saying.

When midday had passed and the guardsmen saw that the deliberation would still not be concluded for a long time, they threw armchains to the ground with a clanking noise and loudly shouted: "Where is the prisoner?" The crowd's anger suddenly rose with the force of a landslide or the crash of waves. Grasping and snapping the (platform) railings with a wrenching noise, they attacked. In the twinkling of an eye the guardsmen and the battalion commanders all were clasping their heads and slinking away to east or west, climbing trees or scrambling up onto buildings. Some hid in privies. Some concealed themselves

with brambles. When the crowd caught them, they all smote their
foreheads and begged for their lives. They suffered severe bodily
injuries; not one was able to escape. One clambered over the wall
to get away, but the people outside the wall flogged him still more
mercilessly. Someone kicked him with wooden clogs until his teeth
were knocked into his throat, and he promptly died.[47]

Now the censor-in-chief, the censor, the supervisor of defenses,
the prefect, and the magistrate no longer consulted one another, and
the students saw that matters were already lost. All scattered to get
away. But amidst the scuffling and confusion the censor-in-chief's
secretaries arrived with officers leading mounted troops. One soldier
began threatening with a sword. The crowd was about to wrest away
the sword and use it on the censor-in-chief when the supervisor of
defenses caught the soldier and flogged him to appease the crowd, which
then became somewhat pacified. The prefect (K'ou) Shen and the
magistrate (Ch'en) Wen-jui, who had long had the people's confidence,
then genially asked them to clear away. The crowd obeyed, and the
censor-in-chief departed. Had it not been for the prefect, the magistrate, and the supervisor of defenses, the censor-in-chief might have
been killed that day. All this time the crowd merely gave vent to
spontaneous anger; it had no formulated plan of action. Before anyone
realized it, the affair had got out of control, and no one knew what the
end might be.

["The Ying-t'ien governor, Mao I-lu, and the provincial
inspector, Hsü Chi, memorialized: 'On the fifteenth day of
the third lunar month of this year (April 11, 1626), on receipt
of an edict to the effect that the traitorous official Chou Shun-
ch'ang, who had been erased from the rolls and made a commoner, was to be arrested, we gave orders by night for the
Su-chou prefect K'ou Shen to send the Wu district magistrate
Ch'en Wen-jui to take Shun-ch'ang under arrest to the district
yamen and carefully to guard him pending promulgation (of the
edict). Subsequently we agreed with the imperially-despatched
battalion commanders Chang Ying-lung 張應龍 and Wen Chih-
ping 文之柄 of the Imperial Guard to promulgate (the edict)
at noon on the eighteenth day of the same lunar month (April
14).[48] We (at the appointed time) went together to the
(designated) public office. Along the road literati and commoners surged around our vehicles so that we could not proceed,

and they wrangled so noisily that we could not distinguish what was being said. After we reached the public office, and just as we were promulgating (the edict), clamorous literati and commoners, despite our cries, surged in with intense noise and great hubbub. Affairs got out of control. We ministers concealed ourselves in self defense and then led the local officials threatening them with punishments and awing them with the imperial authority. But their force, like that of rolling thunder or flashing lightning, was almost sufficient to snap trees and lift up poles. Momentarily our hearts and mouths were entirely devoid of wisdom and courage. We were surrounded and hemmed in. The screams were indescribable. We were jostled and struck with great gusto. But we carefully took the traitorous official Chou Shun-ch'ang into custody as before to await being sent away...."' (HTSL 65.7b.)

["The wave minister of the five lakes" reports: "More than five hundred students in formal attire awaited the two dignitaries outside the gate, trembling with anxiety and warning one another not to make a clamor. Soon the two dignitaries arrived. The common people fell prostrate on the ground, and their cries were like rolling thunder or a raging torrent, rumbling so that not a single word could be distinguished. The students Wang Chieh 王 節 (1599-1660),[49] Liu Yü-i 劉羽儀 (chü-jen 1628),[50] and Wen Chen-heng stepped forward, knelt down, and said: 'Chou Li-pu is such a man as can serve as a model for the literati and people. Suddenly he has found disfavor with the powerful eunuch. He has not been criticized by the Censorate or the Offices of Scrutiny, but it is on the basis of insubstantial complaints by the eunuch Li Shih that he has been vexed with this edict and the sending of guardsmen. The common people cry out for justice, ten thousand voices in unison, and wish to die in his place. We students, in studying and emulating Confucius and Mencius, have learned about a good name, purity, honesty, and a sense of shame. But in present-day affairs, those whom the court casts away are worthy and excellent, whereas those who are employed are treacherous and cunning. How can we students have the countenance any longer in green collars to dwell in so vile a world? You honorable gentlemen are the most important ministers in the southeast. If you are unable to propitiate

heaven and console the hearts of the people, we students
must presume to be ashamed!' When they finished speaking
they wept loudly. Outside the gate all wept until they lost
their voices. Even sedan-chair bearers hid their faces and
were unable to stop lamenting. Flowing perspiration covered
the face of the governor, and he was unable to make any
response. But the guardsmen, with the fierceness of tigers,
came from within carrying weapons to push away the crowd.
In harsh voices they said: 'When the Secret Service Office
(Tung ch'ang)[51] takes a man, how dare rats stick their noses
in?' Thereupon (the commoner) Yen P'ei-wei 顏佩韋 and others
pushed forward and demanded: 'Did this edict issue from the
court or from the Secret Service Office?' The guardsmen
abused them saying: 'Promptly cut out their tongues! If
edicts did not issue from the Secret Service Office, who would
issue them?' The commoners, on hearing this, all bared
their arms. They shouted: 'We thought it was an edict from
the Son of Heaven! How is the Secret Service Office able to
arrest our Li-pu!' Forthwith they attacked, rushing by the
thousands to the foot of the platform. Seizing weapons, they
struck out at the guardsmen. For a long time these proud and
overbearing men, surprised beyond all expectation, cowered
in the rear of the hall. Then the commoners followed them in
and could not be checked. More than twenty of the guardsmen
hid behind a partition and jumped over the wall to escape, but
one of the men was killed. The governor was terrified and
urgently groped around for a weapon with which to defend himself. One armored man entered brandishing a sword, and the
common people scattered in all directions, crying: 'His
Honor has deployed troops who are going to kill us all!' They
tried to outdo one another in throwing tiles and stones, which
were as thick as flying locusts. They were about to panic again
when the supervisor of defenses Chang Hsiao grasped the armored
man and flogged him, whereupon they all settled down. The
prefect K'ou Shen, who had long been popular, again and again
ordered them to clear away. But only deep in the night did they
gradually disperse." (T'i-ch'i chi-lüeh, pp. 29a-30a.)]

[Yin Hsien-ch'en reports: "Early on the eighteenth day
(April 14) the guardsmen demanded money even more urgently,
and the crowd became increasingly angry. At this time the sun

tucked away its brilliance, and a heavy rain filled the air --
as if (heaven) were drinking tears on Chou's behalf. At noon
Chou emerged from the district yamen. Common people
lined the road, holding incense. The sound of the weeping
penetrated the clouds. From the district yamen to the guardsmen's compound their shoulders rubbed and their feet touched.
The vehicles of the governor, the provincial inspector, the
prefect, and the district magistrate were unable to proceed.
Wherever they went people blocked the road and cried out:
'We wish to rescue our Chou!' There even were those who
swore to have vengeance! Then Wang Chieh, Liu Yü-i, Sha
Shun-ch'en 沙舜臣 ,[52] Wang Ching-kao 王景暴 , Wen Chen-heng,
Tsou Ku 鄒谷 ,[53] Wu Er-chang 吳爾璋 ,[54] and Chu Tsu-wen
spoke out obstinately before the two dignitaries, begging that
they say something in (Chou's) defense.[55] Their words and
manner were very provocative. Five men in the rear, Yen
P'ei-wei and others, bared their arms and shouted: 'If Chou
should die, the people also would not wish to live!' They
snatched whips from the guardsmen and turned against them.
The guardsmen, terrified, said: 'Actually, it isn't an imperial
edict. It merely issued from the gentleman Wei.' The five men,
with flashing eyes, angrily said: 'It actually isn't the idea of

the Son of Heaven! Let's all attack these false-edict bearers!'
Thereupon, like the swarming of bees or the gathering of clouds
everyone plucked up his courage and pressed forward. Subsequently there came about an uprising such as a thousand
antiquities never experienced. Meanwhile, Chou prostrated
himself at the middle gate of the yamen and, changing color,
said: 'Grants of kindness and cruelty are entirely the prerogatives of the ruler. The common people have gone insane!
My person is not worthy of being begrudged. If calamity is
brought upon the whole area, what will the literati and people
do?' I myself was thinking, moreover, that Chou's punishment
would be increased; from the midst of the crowd I urgently
cried out: 'Don't!' But I was struck in the face with incense
by madmen and got a good taste of their fists. The affair got
completely out of control, so that law and order could not be
enforced. Consequently there actually was no promulgation."
(Chou Chung-chieh kung nien-p'u, pp. 18b-19b.)

[Chin Jih-sheng reports: "On the eighteenth (April 14) Li-pu in prisoner's garb emerged to await promulgation of the edict. (Yen) P'ei-wei passed around incense and swore oaths with the crowd. He wept in the marketplace and said: 'Those who wish to protect Chou Li-pu follow me!' A very strong man with whom he had formerly associated, Ma Chieh 馬傑 , had already in the morning struck a watchman's rattle and cried out summonses. All at once those who grasped incense and followed were more than ten thousand men. In the rain it was like an array of torches. Arriving at the guardsmen's compound, they saw that fetters had been set up, and the manner of the guardsmen was very arrogant. (Yen P'ei-) wei forthwith led on to the two dignitaries and complained about the injustice to Li-pu. He wished to take his place. Yang Nien-ju 楊念如 , whose former business was selling clothes, and the wholesaler Shen Yang 沈揚 , although they had long loved righteousness, had not been acquainted with Li-pu, nor had they been acquainted with P'ei-wei. But at this time, together with the crowd, they sought to petition so that (Chou) might escape arrest. The sound of their weeping was like the collapse of a mountain. At the corner of the city wall they knelt and begged until noon without getting up. The guardsmen became angry. Then (Ma) Chieh from the side bared his arms and cursed Wei Chung-hsien incessantly. The guardsmen said: 'We will cut out your tongue!' Then they threw arm-chains down on the steps and cried loudly: 'Where is the prisoner?' The crowd raised a great clamor, saying: 'This is a forged edict from the Secret Service Office; how can it be?' The guardsmen started to clap Shen Yang into fetters. Li-pu's sedan-chair bearer, Chou Wen-yüan 周文元 , who after hearing of (Chou's) disaster had wept and cursed for three days without eating, now strode forward and snatched away the fetters, and a guardsman injured him on the forehead. Thereupon the crowd raised a roar like that of a mountain falling into the sea and fought with the black-uniformed men. It went beyond all expectations; they were all injured and scurried away like rats! One man hid in the rafters of the building, but was in such agitation that he fell. Nien-ju promptly attacked and killed him. One man, in getting over the wall, fell to the ground. Someone kicked him in the brain with wooden clogs, and he also died. The censor-in-chief, unable to exert control, finally deployed troops to protect himself. "[56] (Wu-jen chuan, pp. 28a-29a.)]

[Huang Yü (?) reports: ".... It happened to be raining, and
those who had come all had umbrellas and wore wooden clogs.
As their shouts shook the earth, ten thousand wooden clogs
were flung in unison from below the platform...." (Jen-pien
shu-lüeh, p. 42b.)

When late afternoon came, it happened that guardsmen who were
going to Che (-chiang) to arrest Huang Tsun-su passed beneath the
city wall in boats. On arriving at the courier station, they heard that
in the city there had been an uprising; but, not believing this was so,
they made forcible demands as always. The courier station attendants,
already contemptuous, arrogantly ignored them. The guardsmen
became angry and cursed them. They cursed back. (The guardsmen)
angrily struck them. They struck back. When guardsmen who had
gone into the marketplace to buy wine and meats tried to dictate prices,
the market people also grasped and struck them. Moreover, they ran
around on the city wall, crying: "More guardsmen have come!" Thereupon the crowd all responded; they went to the Hsü 胥 river at the foot of
the city wall, burned the boats, and tossed the baggage into the river.
The imperial warrants that had been given (to the guardsmen) were
consequently lost and could not be located. In great distress, the
guardsmen all struggled across the river to the west bank, but many
farmers on the west bank chased them, using rakes and hoes for clubs.
The guardsmen, born and reared in the north, had never become accustomed to water. Clutching bits of wood, they floated several miles
away to a secluded place before daring to emerge. They all suffered
extremely. [57]

["The company commander Chang Kuo-tung 張國棟 of the
Imperial Guard memorialized: 'This officer and Shih Tsung-
pang 史宗邦 were leading guardsmen to arrest Huang Tsun-su
when, on passing through the Su-chou region, we learned that
within the city relatives of Chou Shun-ch'ang had aroused a
rebellion and assembled a crowd. Many persons came out of the
city, obstructed us, rebelliously beat us almost to death, and
tossed us into the river. They also snatched away our imperial
documents and warrants and our clothing and destroyed all.
We were severely injured. We begged the local prefect, one
K'ou, to make an investigation, but six guardsmen could not

be found. We went confusedly on, but when we reached the
P'ing-wang 平望 bridge we were again attacked by a crowd
of villains. Without a route (by which to proceed), we were
only able to borrow a small boat and flee for our lives.
Having fled into the capital (Nanking?) by little-used routes,
we now report. '" (HTSL 65. 17a. )]

When the crowd finally scattered, dusk had come. Only with even-
ing did the sky clear; the moonlight was as bright as daylight. The prefect and the district magistrate sent men into the (guardsmen's) compound to help up the wounded and bruised from amidst the blood and
flesh. All were gasping for breath, and when they heard a voice of the
slightest harshness they shuddered with fear and implored salvation. The
censor-in-chief then issued orders summoning troops in armor from
the (Su-chou) Guard to surround the compound for protection; and Shun-
ch'ang in this one night was repeatedly moved from yamen to yamen.
Shun-ch'ang by now lacked any hope of returning alive, and only one
death is sufficient for a thousand eternities!

The next day was clear. The leading personages of Wu, wearing
white mourning clothes because of the extraordinary incident, called on
the two dignitaries and the supervisor of defenses, seeking some means
of restoring peace to the area. The censor-in-chief had already, in the
night, summoned the censor to his palace, and by lamplight they had
drafted a memorial reporting the uprising.[58] At the fifth watch they
had hurriedly sent it out. Toward the local personages their attitude
was very hateful. They said: "This rebellious crowd! If you gentlemen
had early issued a single word, they would have been soothed! It seems
to us that you gentlemen actually caused it!"

The memorial having been submitted, they secretly sent word to
the local authorities that they wished to obtain the ringleaders for
retribution. Thereupon, because of suspicions, thirteen men, Yen
P'ei-wei and others,[59] were arrested and imprisoned. Case records
were hastily prepared, saying: "Such a one sounded a watchman's
rattle and called out summonses;" "such a one distributed incense and
swore oaths with the crowd;" "such ones are village bullies who assisted
one another in doing evil;" and "the warlike shouts and loud summonses
of such a one were heard far and near." All these things were imaginary
and had not been. At the extreme, there even were various men who
had left (the city?) beforehand and returned afterwards and yet were

still seized. In the trials there was not a single word in self-defense. (The victims) merely said: "When such a worthy as Chou Li-pu comes to such disaster, we little people must certainly die for him; what more is to be said?" They all entered prison chatting and laughing.

The censor-in-chief submitted three memorials within ten days, wishing to exonerate himself through merit in capturing the rebellious leaders. His memorials were increasingly secret, but censors leaked out a little of them. He said: "These men all took the lead because of selfish motives; there was no public indignation." This was in order to substantiate (Li Shih's previous) statement that the people of Wu were gnashing their teeth in profound anger (against Chou and others).60 There was, after all, not a single word about the crying out against injustice. Everyone said that the censor-in-chief's heart had already been dead for a long time, and the crowd swore to prevent Shun-ch'ang's arrest even to death. Rumors appeared on all sides, and placards were posted in the thoroughfares, saying that the crowd must die along with him. Thereupon the prefect and the magistrate both went to Shun-ch'ang and plotted to let it be known that he would not be sent away pending imperial action. But suddenly one night troops were sent out to take up positions on water and on land, and (Chou) was secretly despatched to undertake his journey. The battalion commanders and the guardsmen who were lucky enough to remain alive all were happy to get out the Chin-ch'ang 金閶 gate61 with their lives. The prefect and the magistrate proceeded in a small boat together with Shun-ch'ang. Only when they had crossed the domestic-customs barrier and anchored in a wilderness did they dare to proclaim the edict. Thus crudely was the matter terminated. When daylight came and the crowd learned of this, Shun-ch'ang was already long gone.62

Meantime Chung-hsien's spies in Wu hurried along by-roads by swift night courier to the capital (literally, Ch'ang-an) to report the uprising. (The first) said: "Chiang-nan is in revolt! The guardsmen have all been killed!" The next to arrive said: "Shun-ch'ang has been liberated, and flags have been set up over the city gates. The gates are closed in daylight!" The next to arrive said: "The censor-in-chief has already been killed! The transport routes have been blocked and the transport boats plundered."

Chung-hsien on hearing these things was very frightened. He blamed (Ts'ui) Ch'eng-hsiu. He made him kneel down and reprimanded

him, saying: "You told me to arrest all of these five men, and now
rebellion has been aroused in the southeast. The southeast is the area
from which (great) revenues are levied. If they are lost, how can we
later accomplish great things?" Ch'eng-hsiu was terrified; he knocked
his head and begged for death. Chung-hsien abusively sent him away.
Ch'eng-hsiu, in great distress, wished to hang himself, but members
of his household encircled him and prevented it.

When Li Shih heard of the uprising, he locked his gate and wept
until his eyes swelled completely to.

When the censor-in-chief's (first) memorial arrived, the chief
minister, originally a man of Wu, [63] was so shocked he was unable to
get out. The secondary minister[64] undertook to substitute for him in
drafting a rescript. Chung-hsien went to the Secretariat and, with a
fierce countenance, said: "The Emperor is thunderously angry; he
will certainly wish to put to death all those who have rebelled." The
secondary minister said: "The gentleman is surely mistaken! The
capital looks to Chiang-nan for the transport of grain by the millions
(of piculs). Now the transport season is at hand, and the area is in
revolt. Properly, lenience and magnanimity should be displayed. If
it is further aroused through stern edicts, with the result that there are
other losses, then who will bear the blame?" Chung-hsien went back
into (the palace) without answering.

The Secretariat minister who was newest in the administration[65]
alone thought differently. When the rescript was being drafted, he
grasped the memorial from the hand of the secondary minister, took
up a pen, and started to write. But the train of his thoughts suddenly
became very vague, and he was unable to compose a single statement.
Chung-hsien urged him on; but the secondary minister took back the
memorial and wrote: "There has been received a rescript, stating:
'When Shun-ch'ang is brought in under arrest, the court naturally will
deliberate about disposition of him. How can little people, lacking in
knowledge, press in crowds and cry out so as to cause a great clamor?
If they disperse at once, there need not be a thorough investigation'" and
so forth. In general, it clearly indicated that the governor and the
provincial inspector should terminate the matter by means of a lenient
policy. [66]

As soon as the censor-in-chief's second memorial arrived, there was received a rescript stating: "The common people have gone so wild as to form a mob and injure guardsmen."[67] There was still no desire to apply to this the designation of murdering an imperial envoy. But when the censor-in-chief's third memorial arrived, it stated: "I have caught the violent people who incited the trouble, and the area is submissive." Moreover, it included such statements as "none has escaped the net of heaven" and "public opinion is all aroused."[68] Chung-hsien consequently said: "This being the case, then let us no longer worry about inciting rebellion." It now happened that the secondary minister fell ill and died, and the chief minister came forth to take charge of affairs. He humbly took orders (from Wei Chung-hsien). Thereupon there was issued an edict about the chief rebels who had escaped the net, and the commander of the Imperial Guard, T'ien Er-keng 田爾耕 (d. 1628),[69] subsequently memorialized about the students. A former censor jestingly said to a man of Wu who held office in the capital: "Is Chou Li-pu, then, truly another Lord of Fu-yü ( 扶餘國主 )?"[70] This was because he profoundly hated him.

In Wu, meanwhile, there was wild terror day and night. It was said that there were going to be pit-burials (of literati) and massacres (of commoners), and rich families all moved away.[71] In the deliberations of the inner court, it was insistently desired that great trials be undertaken in the three Wu (i.e., Su-chou, Ch'ang-chou, and Hu-chou prefectures), beginning with the students who had spoken out in opposition. Moreover, guardsmen had reported their names, and they had already been arrested!

Just at the time when Chung-hsien and his partisans were secretly plotting in the palace, there was a sudden earthquake.[72] A roof ornament over the place where they were sitting fell without any apparent reason, and two young eunuchs whom (Wei) favored were crushed to death. In a moment there was a sound like thunder rising from the northwest. It shook heaven and earth, and black clouds flowed over confusedly. People's dwellings were destroyed to such an extent that for several miles (li) nothing remained. Great stones hurtled down from the sky like rain. Men and women died by the tens of thousands; donkeys, horses, chickens, and dogs all had broken or cracked limbs. People with smashed skulls or broken noses were strewn about -- the streets were full of them! Gunpowder that had previously been stored in the Imperial Arsenal (Wang kung ch'ang)[73] exploded. This alarmed elephants, [74] and the elephants ran about wildly, trampling to death an incalculable number of people.

The court astrologer reported his interpretation of these events as follows: "In the earth there is tumultuous noise. This is an evil omen of calamity in the world. When noise gushes forth from within the earth, the city must be destroyed." He also said: "The reason why the earth growls is that throughout the empire troops arise to attack one another and that palace women and eunuchs have brought about great disorder." Chung-hsien promptly beat him to death. How far more worthy was this court astrologer, who though a minor minister was yet able obstinately to remonstrate about a technical matter, than those who sang praises of (Wei's) merits and virtues!

When the calamity subsided, the commander of the Imperial Guard made further requests about the Wu affair, but Chung-hsien had been awed by the disaster and ordered that the matter be set aside for the time being. [75] Yet in the end Shun-ch'ang died in prison. [76] Till death he cursed incessantly. When it was produced in a mixed-up group, his corpse was so mutilated that it could no longer be identified. Even passers-by were deeply moved.

Further, there was issued an edict secretly ordering the censor-in-chief immediately to put to death five men including Yen P'ei-wei and to send others into frontier military service. The education intendant was also ordered to degrade or dismiss the students, variably. Their names have been recorded elsewhere. [77] The censor-in-chief, afraid of inciting another uprising, did not dare carry out the executions publicly. He turned the victims in fetters over to the supervisor of defenses, who, with tears flowing freely, beheaded them in front of the guardsmen's compound. [78]

One day before the executions there were again fierce winds and heavy rains, as when Shun-ch'ang was arrested. Trees were uprooted and stalks of grain were killed. The water of the Grand Lake (T'ai-hu) was churned up so that it inundated people's thatched huts, and those who drowned were innumerable. The Yangtze River overflowed for several days and nights. People all said this had been brought about by (heaven's) resentment. [79]

Knowing that Chung-hsien and Ch'eng-hsiu, when plotting to arrest

and put to death all the various partisans, actually gave first consideration to Wu, guardsmen in advance gave several thousand (taels of) silver
to the commander of the Imperial Guard in the hope of making the arrests
one after another and in the expectation that, after obtaining the commis-
sions, they might make extortionate demands without restraint. But
beginning with the affair in Wu, the wrath of heaven and the anger of men
reacted upon and responded to one another. Chung-hsien became cautious
and the guardsmen warned one another not to dare to go south. The
imperial warrant for Huang Tsun-su being already lost, there was
enacted nothing more than an arrest by the governor and the provincial
inspector. [80]

All over the empire it was said that the attack in Wu was comparable
to the bludgeoning (of the tyrannical ancient Emperor Ch'in Shih Huang,
attempted) at Po-lang 博浪 . [81]

1. Chu Yu-chiao, b. 1605, reigned under the <u>nien-hao</u> T'ien-ch'i.
See article "Chu Yu-chiao" by George A. Kennedy in A. W. Hummel, ed.,
<u>Eminent Chinese of the Ch'ing Period (1644-1912)</u> (2 vols., Washington,
1943-1944).

2. See article "Wei Chung-hsien" by George A. Kennedy in A. W.
Hummel, <u>op. cit.</u>, and <u>Ming-shih</u> (T'ung-wen edition), 305. 18a-28a.
(<u>Ming-shih</u> is hereinafter cited as MS.) Wei was degraded and banished
after the death of Hsi Tsung in 1627; and, when further punishment was
being planned, he finally committed suicide.

3. The best modern survey of the late Ming partisan struggle is
Hsieh Kuo-chen, <u>Ming Ch'ing chih chi tang-she yün-tung k'ao</u> (Shanghai,
Commercial Press, 1934). Also see Ch'en Ting, ed., <u>Tung-lin lieh-</u>
<u>chuan</u> (26 chüan, 1711 edition); <u>Tung-lin shu-yüan chih</u> (22 chüan, 1882
edition); and Wen Ping, <u>Hsien-po chih-shih</u> (Chieh-yüeh shan-fang hui-
<u>ch'ao</u> edition). For a survey of the extensive Chinese literature on this
subject, see Hsieh Kuo-chen, <u>Wan Ming shih-chi k'ao</u> (20 chüan, Peking,
1932).

4. Chu I-chün, b. 1563, reigned under the <u>nien-hao</u> Wan-li.

5. For biographical data about Chou Shun-ch'ang, see MS 245.5a-
6b; Wen Ping, <u>Ku-su ming-hsien hsü-chi</u> (Chia-hsü ts'ung-pien edition),
p. 7a; Miao Ching-ch'ih, <u>Tung-lin t'ung-nan tu</u> (Yen-hua-tung t'ang hsiao-
p'in edition), 1.26a-26b, 2.30b-32a; and Yin Hsien-ch'en, <u>Chou Chung-</u>
<u>chieh kung nien-p'u</u> (Chieh-yüeh shan-fang hui-ch'ao edition).

6. See Wen Ping, <u>Hsien-po chih-shih</u>, 2.21b; Chin Jih-sheng, <u>Chou</u>
<u>Shun-ch'ang chuan,</u> in <u>Sung-t'ien lu-pi</u> (24 chüan, preface dated 1629),
8.1a. While serving in the Ministry of Civil Service, Chou once rebuked
a subordinate for offering him a dose of ginseng and insisted upon paying
for it. See Chi Liu-ch'i, <u>Ming-chi pei-lüeh</u> (Kuo-hsüeh chi-pen ts'ung-
<u>shu</u> edition), vol. 1, p. 37 (chüan 2).

7. MS 245.5a-6b.

8. Yin Hsien-ch'en, <u>op. cit.</u>, pp. 11a-11b; <u>Tung-lin shu-yüan chih,</u>

22.37b. The imperial rescript that ordered Chou's arrest did classify him as an Eastern Forest partisan. See Hsi Tsung shih-lu (1940 photo-lithographic edition), 63.35b. But two sources report that in 1624, when partisans of Wei Chung-hsien prepared a blacklist of Eastern Forest partisans called Tung-lin tien-chiang lu, Chou's name (and he considered this shameful) was omitted. See Chang Shih-wei, Chou Li-pu chi-shih (see note 15), p. 19b; and Jen-pien shu-lüeh (see note 30). Almost all of the extant texts of Tung-lin tien-chiang lu nevertheless include Chou's name. See Chu Tan, "Tung-lin tien-chiang lu k'ao-i" in Kuo-li Chung-shan ta-hsüeh wen-shih-hsüeh yen-chiu so yüeh-k'an, vol. 2, no. 1 (October, 1933), pp. 33-65.

9. See Pei-ching jen-wen k'o-hsüeh yen-chiu so ts'ang-shu mu-lu (8 vols., Peking, 1938), vol. 6, p. 19a, where this collection is identified as a manuscript of the Ming period. It is now in the possession of the Academia Sinica Institute of History and Philology in Taiwan.

10. The modern scholar Hsieh Kuo-chen (Wan Ming shih-chi k'ao, 5.18a) attributes authorship of this work to Chin Jih-sheng; but this appears to be an assumption, not a considered judgment, derived from the attribution of editorship of the item to Chin in Pi-ts'e ts'ung-shuo. Inclusion of the work in Sung-t'ien lu-pi does not seem of itself to be satisfactory evidence of Chin's authorship, since many items not of Chin's authorship are included in this compilation. Appended to the Sung-tien lu-pi text is an uninformative postface signed merely with the pseudonym "the lonely man of Wu (吳市門畸人)." The seventeenth-century Su-chou author Ku Ling, however, in a biographical notice of his friend Wen Chen-heng that has been published in Ku-su ming-hsien hou-chi (I-hai ts'ung-pien edition), pp. 23b-24b, lists K'ai-tu ch'uan-hsin among the published works of Wen. Wen was among the close friends of Chou Shun-ch'ang; one of his nephews married one of Chou's daughters. See Su-chou fu chih (160 chüan, 1824 edition), 90.30b-31a (biography of Wen Ch'eng). And since several independent texts (e.g., those of Yin Hsien-ch'en and "the wave minister of the five lakes") confirm the fact of Wen's participation in the demonstration against Chou's arrest, it is clear that he could have written a detailed eye-witness account of it. Strong support for the contention that Wen actually did write K'ai-tu ch'uan-hsin derives from the considerations that (1) Wen is the only "student" participant identified therein, and (2) K'ai-tu ch'uan-hsin credits Wen with long and heroic statements addressed to the authorities over the promulgation ceremony, whereas (3) no

independent text goes beyond mere mention of Wen as one of several
persons who addressed the authorities, and (4) Wen was in fact not
among the five students who were subsequently degraded for having
been ringleaders in the demonstration.  It appears impossible, nevertheless, clearly to identify Wen with "the lonely man of Wu" of the
Sung-t'ien lu-pi text.

11. Yin Hsien-ch'en, a resident of Su-chou, compiled Chou Chung-
chieh kung nien-p'u (see note 5).  Yin was among Chou Shun-ch'ang's
close friends and a participant in the 1626 demonstration, although his
biography of Chou does not give a detailed chronicle of the incident.
When the Ming dynasty fell, he starved himself to death.  One of his
sons married one of Chou's daughters.  See Su-chou fu chih, 90.32b;
Hsü Tzu, Hsiao-t'ien chi-chuan (1887 edition), 49.5b; and Miao Ching-
ch'ih, op. cit., 3.7b-8a.

12. Chu Tsu-wen, a student of Su-chou, was indebted to Chou for
help in obtaining official recognition of the virtues of his widowed
mother.  He was in Chou's company almost without a break from the
time of Chou's arrest until his departure from Su-chou.  Chu escorted
Chou out of the city, then preceded him to Peking, and ruined his
health trying to raise money for Chou's cause in the north.  After Chou's
death, Chu fell ill and soon died.  During his illness he compiled a
diary for the period beginning with Chou's arrest, Pei-hsing jih-p'u,
included in Chih-pu-tsu chai ts'ung-shu, series 21.  For biographical
data, see Chin Jih-sheng, Chu Wen-hsüeh, in Sung-t'ien lu-pi, 22.26a-
27b; Su-chou fu chih, 92.25a-25b; and MS 245.7a.

13. Yang T'ing-shu, who attained the degree of chü-jen and was
first on the list in the provincial examination of 1630, was a man of
great literary renown, a founder of the Ying-she        literary society
and of the massive Fu-she ("antiquity-restoration society") literary-
political movement into which it grew, and a famous teacher who is
said to have taught two thousand identified students.  He supported his
friend Chou Shun-ch'ang during the 1626 demonstration and wrote a
brief account of it entitled Ch'üan Wu chi-lüeh, included in Ching-t'o
i-shih.  After the fall of the Ming dynasty he became a recluse.  Finally
caught by the Manchus and ordered to adopt the Manchu hair style, he
refused and was put to death.  For biographical and background inform-
ation, see MS 267.11a-12a; Su-chou fu chih, 90.13a-14a; Wu-hsien chih
(1933 edition), 69A.14b-15a; Chu Tan, "Ming-chi nan Ying-she k'ao,"

in Kuo-hsüeh chi-k'an, vol 2, no. 3(September, 1930), pp. 541-588; and entry entitles "Chang P'u" in A.W. Hummel, op. cit.

14.  See Chin Jih-sheng, Chou Shun-ch'ang chuan. Whether or not Chin witnessed the 1626 incident is not specifically stated.

15.  Chang Shih-wei, a resident of Su-chou and a close friend of Chou, is said to have done much to stir up indignation over Chou's arrest; it appears almost certain that he witnessed the demonstration of which he wrote vividly in Chou Li-pu cho-shih, printed in Sung-t'ien lu-pi, 8. 4a-21b. For biographical data see Su-chou fu-chih, 92. 22b-23a; Chu I-tsun, Ming-shih tsung (100 chüan, 1705 edition), 70. 4a-4b. Chang attained the chü-jen degree in 1612.

16.  Yao Hsi-meng was a chin-shih of 1619, a supporter of the Eastern Forest Party, a nephew of Wen Chen-heng, and a life-long associate of Wen's older brother Wen Chen-meng (1547-1636). After an influential career in the Han-lin yüan at Peking, he returned home in mourning in 1625 and was soon erased from the rolls. He was one of Chou Shun-ch'ang's most intimate friends; but he was absent from Su-chou at the time of Chou's arrest (see Ts'ai Shih-shun, Li Chung-ta pei-tai chi-lüeh [Ching-t'o i-shih edition], pp. 1a-1b) and appears to have remained absent until after Chou's departure, for Chou hoped to meet him enroute (see second letter from Chou to Yao in Chou Chung-chieh kung chin-yü chi [Chieh-yüeh shan-fang hui-ch'ao edition, 4 chüan], 2. 18a-18b). His account of the 1626 incident, K'ai-tu shih-mo, appears in his collected works, Yao Meng-chang ch'üan-chi (54 chüan, Ch'ung-chen edition), in the section Kung-huai chi (6 chüan), 3. 11a-16b. It was republished, with minor variations and without attribution of authorship, in Wu-hsien chih, 78. 21b-23a, ascribed to an early gazetteer of the K'ang-hsi period (1662-1722). This account differs substantially fron K'ai-tu ch'uan-hsin, but in many places the wording is identical.

17. T'i-ch'i chi-lüeh appears in Sung-t'ien lu-pi, 21. 22a-34b (listed in the table of contents as T'i-ch'i shu but in chüan 21 as above), and in

Pi-ts'e ts'ung-shuo, vol. 13, pp. 9a-14b. "The wave minister of the five lakes" remains unidentified, but inclusion of this item in Sung-tien lu-pi would appear to give it some authority, and perhaps the authority of an eyewitness account, considering its vivid detail. (Subsequent citations are of the Sung-t'ien lu-pi text.)

18. Official documents relating to the Su-chou incident include the following:
　(1) Memorial by Mao I-lu and Hsü Chi abstracted in HTSL (i.e., Hsi-tsung shih-lu), 65.7b-8a (under date 1626.4 丙子)
　(2) Memorial by Mao I-lu and Hsü Chi abstracted in HTSL 65.16a-17a (1626.4);
　(3) Memorial by Chang Kuo-tung abstracted in HTSL 65.17a-17b (1626.4);
　(4) Memorial by Mao I-lu abstracted in HTSL 68.25a-25b (1626.6a);
　(5) Memorial by Mao I-lu quoted in Li Hsün-chih, San-ch'ao yeh-chi (Ching-t'o i-shih edition), 3A.36a-36b (identical with #4?); and
　(6) Hsü hsün-an chieh-t'ieh (Memorial by Hsü Chi, dated 1626.6) in Yu-man lou ts'ung-shu, vol. 1.

19. Wei Ta-chung, a man of Chia-shan district in Chekiang, south of Su-chou, was a chin-shih of 1616, and served thereafter in the capital as messenger and supervising secretary, becoming in 1624 chief supervising secretary of the Office of Scrutiny for Civil Service. Closely allied with the Eastern Forest Party, he was one of the most outspoken critics of Wei Chung-hsien and his henchmen. Consequently, he was among the famous "six heroes" who were arrested and put to death in prison in 1625. See MS 244.15b-19a and entry entitled "Yang Lien" in A.W. Hummel, op. cit.

20. Cf. HTSL 56.8b-9a, under date 1625.7 壬戌 Ni was one of the most active of Wei Chung-hsien's adherents. After he had previously caused the death of the censor Hsia Chih-ling 夏之令 , Chou Shun-ch'ang said publicly that Ni one day would have to pay with his own life for Hsia's. Ni consequently hated Chou. See MS 306.18b-19a, 245.5b; and Yang-chou fu chih (73 chüan, 1810 edition), 39.22b.

21. Cf. Su-chou fu chih, 72.20a; Wu-hsien chih, 63.30b.

22. Li Shih entered palace service in 1578. Most sources describe him as being illiterate (e.g., Wen Ping, Hsien-po chih-shih, 2.21a),

74

but his fellow-eunuch Liu Jo-yü testified that he had studied the orthodox literature and was a companion-reader to the crown prince under Shen Tsung (Cho-chung chih [24 chüan, Cheng-chüeh lou ts'ung-k'o edition], 15.19a-20a). Under Hsi Tsung, he seems to have lost favor, for he was not originally a partisan of Wei Chung-hsien, and in 1621 he was sent out to be superviser of textile manufactures in Su-chou and Hang-chou. All sources agree that he was coarse and common; but it has been suggested that the Eastern Forest partisan Huang Tsun-su connived with Li in the hope of using him as a tool by means of which the partisans might have palace support in an attempt to overthrow Wei. In the end, however, Li was branded a Wei Chung-hsien partisan. After the death of Hsi Tsung he was demoted to be an inspector of troops at Nanking, where he died of old age. Cf. Wu Ying-chi, Ch'i-chen liang-ch'ao po-fu lu (Kuei-ch'ih hsien-che i-shu edition), 3.5b-6a; MS 245.12a-15b. Regarding the post of superviser of textile manufactures, see MS 74.26b; Liu Jo-yü, op. cit., 16.10b-11a.

23. Chou Ch'i-yüan was a long-time adherent of the Eastern Forest Party. He was appointed governor of the southern metropolitan area (Ying-t'ien and surrounding prefectures) in 1623. See MS 245.1a-3a.

24. This essay is reproduced in full in Chou Chung-chieh kung chin-yü chi, 3.1a-2b. Abbreviated versions are found in Chang Shih-wei, op. cit., p. 6b; and in the biography of Chou Ch'i-yüan in Wu Ying-chi, Hsi-ch'ao chung-chieh ssŭ-ch'en chuan (Ching-t'o i-shih edition), pp. 22a-23a.

25. Mao I-lu, a native of Sui-an district in Chekiang, served as governor of the southern metropolitan area from the second lunar month of 1625 until the tenth lunar month of 1626, when he was promoted to be vice-minister of war. See Ming tu-fu nien-piao (in Er-shih-wu shih pu-pien) p. 134.

26. This was Chu T'ung-meng 朱童蒙 (chin-shih 1610), a long-time opponent of the Eastern Forest Party (e.g., see MS 243.10b-11a) and a favorite of Wei Chung-hsien, who at this time was an official of the (Chekiang?) Provincial Investigation Office. See Li Hsün-chih, op. cit., 3A.1a-1b. (The text here reads 一兵備裏臣 ; Li Hsün-chih more specifically identifies Chu as 蘇松兵備 .) The Ming-shih is apparently mistaken in identifying him as vice-commissioner of the Provincial Administration Office (MS 245.2b: 公守參政 ).

27. Chou Tsung-chien, a man of Wu district and a chin-shih of 1613, was a censor and one of the most outspoken and independent Eastern Forest partisans during the early part of Hsi Tsung's reign. Late in 1623 he went home in mourning. In 1625 he was erased from the rolls, and a full recovery of his alleged bribery-loot was ordered. See MS 245.7b-11b.

28. Miao Ch'ang-ch'i was a resident of Ch'ang-chou prefecture near Su-chou and a chin-shih of 1613. Serving in the Han-lin yüan, he supported Yang Lien's famous attack on Wei Chung-hsien in 1624; the eunuch thought he had actually drafted Yang's memorial. Subsequently Miao was erased from the rolls. See MS 245.3a-5a.

29. Kao P'an-lung, one of the most eminent philosophers of the late Ming era, was a native of Wu-hsi district in Ch'ang-chou prefecture and one of the founders of the Eastern Forest Academy at Wu-hsi. A chin-shih of 1589, he had barely got started on an official career when he became entangled in partisan wrangling and had to retire. Recalled in 1621, he became censor-in-chief but late in 1624 departed on leave of absence. When the order for his arrest arrived in 1626, Kao drowned himself. See MS 243.15b-19b.

30. Li Ying-sheng, another native of Ch'ang-chou prefecture, attained the chin-shin degree in 1616. A censor and another outspoken critic of Wei Chung-hsien, Li was erased from the rolls in 1625. See MS 245.15b-18b. A secondary source reports that when Li was arrested the people of Ch'ang-chou rose up to attack the guardsmen in much the same manner as the people of Su-chou demonstrated on behalf of Chou Shun-ch'ang. See Jen-pien shu-lüeh in Huang Yü, Pi-hsüeh lu (Chih-pu-tsu chai ts'ung-shu, series 13, edition,) 2.40a-44a; quoted in Li Hsün-chih, op. cit., 3A.36b-39b. (An abbreviated version of Jen-pien shu-lüeh appears in Ching-t'o i-shih. Whether or not the work was actually written by Huang Yü, as is indicated in the Ching-t'o i-shih text, is not clear. See Hsieh Kuo-chen, Wan Ming shih-chi k'ao, 5.13b-15a.) But an eyewitness report indicates that Ch'ang-chou authorities, having learned of the incident at Su-chou and knowing that the people of Ch'ang-chou were in a very disturbed mood, prevented trouble by not permitting the public to attend the ceremony at which the order of arrest was promulgated. See Ts'ai Shih-shun, op. cit., p. 2b.

31. Huang Tsun-su was a native of Yü-yao district of Chekiang

province. A <u>chin-shih</u> of 1616, he became a censor and a vigorous opponent of Wei Chung-hsien and was erased from the rolls in 1625. He was the father of the great scholar Huang Tsung-hsi. See MS 245.12a-15b.

32. Cf. HTSL 63.35a-36a (under date 1626.2)

33. Cf. HTSL 63.20b-21a (under date 1626.2)

34. Ts'ui Ch'eng-hsiu was one of the most vicious of Wei Chung-hsien's henchmen. As a censor, he was attacked for corruption by Kao P'an-lung and then in self-defense threw himself on the mercy of Wei and became his adopted son. See MS 306.15b-18a.

35. The five men whose arrests were ordered at this time were Chou Ch'i-yüan, Chou Shun-ch'ang, Kao P'an-lung, Li Ying-sheng, and Huang Tsun-su. The arrests of Chou Tsung-chien and Miao Ch'ang-ch'i had been ordered previously. With the exception of Kao P'an-lung, who committed suicide, all of these men subsequently were put to death in prison.

36. Most sources agree that Li's memorial was prepared in his name by order of Wei Chung-hsien on a blank memorial sheet bearing only Li's seal. The last Ming Emperor satisfied himself that such had been the case from an inspection of the overlapping black and red ink on the original document. It was apparently by permitting use of his name in this manner that Li was himself able to escape Wei's wrath at reports of Li's connivance with Huang Tsun-su. See MS 245.1a-3a; Li Hsün-chih, <u>op. cit.</u>, 3A.35b-36a; Wen Ping, <u>Hsien-po chih-shih</u>, 2.21a; Liu Jo-yü, <u>op. cit.</u>, 15.19a-20a; and Wen Ping, <u>Lieh-huang hsiao-shih,</u> chüan 1, in <u>Ming-chi pai-shih ch'u-pien</u> (<u>Kuo-hsüeh chi-pen ts'ung-shu</u> edition), vol. 1, pp. 12-13. It would appear that the impeachment, whether or not actually submitted by Li, represented Wei's wishes rather than Li's; for all of the men named had offended Wei, whereas not all can be proved to have offended Li.

37. Guardsmen arrived in Su-chou to arrest Chou Tsung-chien on the fifth day of the third lunar month (April 1) of 1626. Their edict was promulgated on the tenth day (April 6), and they departed with Chou on the twelfth day (April 8). On the fifteenth day (April 11) guardsmen arrived to arrest Chou Shun-ch'ang. See Chang Shih-wei, <u>op. cit.</u>, p. 8b. Chou Shun-ch'ang had contributed money to both Chou Tsung-chien and

Miao Ch'ang-ch'i when they were arrested, using funds he had obtained by pawning his official gowns and hats. See Yin Hsien-ch'en, op. cit., p. 15b.

38.  Ch'en Wen-jui had earlier studied under Chou Shun-ch'ang. See Su-chou fu chih, 73.11b-12a; Yin Hsien-ch'en, op. cit., p. 16b; and Chi Liu-ch'i, op. cit., vol. 1, p. 37.

39.  This inscription, reading "small-cloud roost" 小雲樓, was inscribed and signed by Chou on behalf of the Lung-shu monastery outside Su-chou, founded by the monk Kuang Ch'uan 廣傳 and given its name by Chou himself. See Su-chou fu chih, 41.30a-30b, 120.11b-12a; T'i-ch'i chi-lüeh, p. 27b; Yao Hsi-meng, K'ai-tu shih-mo, p. 11b; Yin Hsien-ch'en, op. cit., p. 16b; Jen-pien shu-lüeh, p. 41b; and Chi Liu-ch'i, op. cit., vol. 1, p. 38.

40.  Throughout this text, the term "student" (chu-sheng) refers to a person who at some time had been admitted to a government school at the district level or above. It corresponds generally to the term hsiu-ts'ai of other periods and designated a person's status in the hierarchy of government degrees, not necessarily indicating that he was a young man at the moment studying in a school. Of the various students identified in this and related texts, many were of Chou Shun-ch'ang's generation and thus not youths.

41.  This text identifies the guardsmen's compound as the shih-shu 使署, literally "the envoy's yamen" (?). Other sources identify it as "the western investigation office" (hsi ch'a-yüan). See Chang Shih-wei, op. cit., p. 10a; Yin Hsien-ch'en, op. cit., p. 18b; and T'i-ch'i chi-lüeh, p. 28b. "The western investigation office" was primarily used as a headquarters for the Censorate's inspector of salt production during his visits. See Su-chou fu chih, 22.10a.

42.  A total of sixty men had been sent out by the Imperial Guard, led by the battalion commanders Chang Ying-lung 張應龍 and Wen Chih-ping 文之炳. See Chi Liu-ch'i, op. cit., vol. 1, p. 37; T'i-ch'i chi-lüeh, p. 27a; and Yao Hsi-meng, K'ai-tu shih-mo, p. 11b.

43.  For details of this incident, which occurred in 1483, see Su-chou fu chih, 145.28b-30a; and MS 304.18b-19a, 182.1a-8a. Wang Chih was second in the succession of four great eunuch despots of the Ming dynasty, which culminated with Wei Chung-hsien. See MS 304.13b-

17a.

44. See MS 163. 2b-3a. Wang Chen was the first great eunuch despot of the Ming dynasty. See MS 304. 7b-10a.

45. Cf. Chung-kuo jen-ming ta tz'ŭ-tien (Shanghai, 1934), p. 1761.

46. Cf. Herbert A. Giles, A Chinese Biographical Dictionary (London and Shanghai, 1898), no. 1645.

47. The sources disagree about the number of guardsmen killed in this uprising. One man named Li Kuo-chu 李國柱 is definitely reported to have died. See HTSL 65. 16a-17a; Yao Hsi-meng, K'ai-tu shih-mo, pp. 11a, 13b; and Jen-pien shu-lŭeh, p. 42b. Chin Jih-sheng in Wu-jen chuan (Sung-t'ien lu-pi, 22. 28a-30b; reproduced in chŭan 4 of Chou Chung-chieh kung chin-yŭ chi) says two men died, and this assertion is repeated in MS 305. 23a.

48. In their second memorial, Mao I-lu and Hsŭ Chi blamed the guardsmen for the three-day delay, without which they said the incident would not have occurred. See HTSL 65. 16a-17a.

49. Wang Chieh, a resident of Wu district, became a chŭ-jen in 1639. For brief biographical data see Miao Ching-ch'ih, op. cit., 3. 8b-9a.

50. Liu Yŭ-i, also a resident of Wu district, was an intimate friend of Chou Shun-ch'ang. See Miao Ching-ch'ih, op. cit., 3. 7a-7b.

51. The Tung ch'ang was a eunuch-controlled agency which, in cooperation with the Imperial Guard, provided a kind of secret service for the Emperor. See MS 74. 26a.

52. Sha Shun-ch'en, a resident of Su-chou, was renowned for his filial piety. See Su-chou fu chih, 92. 27a-27b; and Miao Ching-ch'ih, op. cit., 3. 7b.

53. See Miao Ching-ch'ih, op. cit., 3. 8a-8b.

54. Wu Er-chang was an uncle of Chou Shun-ch'ung's wife. See Chi Liu-ch'i, op. cit., vol. 1, p. 37.

55. Still other students who are said to have participated in this demonstration include: Yang T'ing-shu (see note 13); Liu Shu 劉曙 (d. 1647, chin-shih 1643; see Su-chou fu chih, 90. 21b-22a; and Hsü Tzu, Hsiao-t'ien chi-chuan, 49. 19b-20a); Cheng Fu-chiao 鄭敷教 (chü-jen 1630, later one of the founders of the "antiquity-restoration society"; see Su-chou fu chih, 99. 41b-42a); Yin Hsien-ch'en himself; Yüan Cheng 袁徵 (see Chu I-tsun, op. cit., 76. 24b); Chu Wei 朱隗 (another member of the "antiquity-restoration society"; see Su-chou fu chih, 99. 42a; and Chu I-tsun, op. cit., 76. 4a); and Wang I-ching 王一經 . See Chi Liu-ch'i, op. cit., vol. 1, p. 38.

56. Hsü Chi's memorial generally substantiates this description of the activities of these five commoners. According to him, Yen P'ei-wei, who was then thirty-four years old and was chief leader of the uprising, passed around incense and swore oaths with the crowd. Ma Chieh struck a watchman's rattle and shouted summonses. Shen Yang also incited the crowd. Yang Nien-ju and Chou Wen-yüan bared their arms, cried out wildly, and fought with the guardsmen. See Hsü hsün-an chieh-t'ieh. Chin Jih-sheng notes that Yen P'ei-wei came of a mercantile family. See Wu-jen chuan, p. 28a. Two days before the promulgation ceremony, Yen P'ei-wei had attacked a district functionary who had made abusive remarks about Chou Shun-ch'ang. See Yin Hsien-ch'en, op. cit., p. 17b.

57. Cf. T'i-ch'i chi-lüeh, pp. 30b-31a; Yao Hsi-meng, K'ai-tu shih-mo, pp. 13b-14a; and Yin Hsien-ch'en, op. cit., p. 19b. Jen-pien shu-lüeh, p. 43a, says that the crowd, after disposing of this new group of guardsmen, proposed traveling about to find and kill the eunuch Li Shih and to wipe out the family of the chief Secretariat minister, Ku Ping-ch'ien 顧秉謙 , but was deterred by Yen P'ei-wei. Hsü Chi says that when these guardsmen arrived and made extravagant demands at the courier station, the courier station attendant Yang Fang 楊芳 complained and shouted wildly for help; that the butcher Tai Yung 戴鏞
raised a clamor over the guardsmen's attempts to dictate prices in the marketplace; that Hsü Er-ch'eng 許爾成 , Chi Mao-hsün 季卯孫 , and Ting K'uei 丁奎 thereupon summoned Yen P'ei-wei and others from the city; and that the crowd reached the courier station in a boat provided by the courier station attendant Tsou Ying-chen 鄒應禎. See Hsü hsün-an chieh-t'ieh.

58. This memorial is abstracted in HTSL 65. 7b-8a.

59. The thirteen commoners who were arrested were Yen P'ei-wei, Ma Chieh, Shen Yang, Yang Nien-ju, and Chou Wen-yüan, all subsequently put to death; Wu Shih-hsin 吳時信 (active in the attack at the guardsmen's compound), Liu Ying-wen 劉應文 (active at the guardsmen's compound), Ting K'uei (active both at the guardsmen's compound and at the courier station), Hsü Er-ch'eng, and Chi Mao-hsün, all subsequently banished to frontier military service; Tsou Ying-chen and Yang Fang, both subsequently given sixty blows with the bastinado; and the butcher Tai Yung, who died after his arrest. See Hsü hsün-an chieh-t'ieh; and HTSL 68.25a-25b.

60. Cf. Yao Hsi-meng, K'ai-tu shih-mo, p. 14b: "He said: 'These men all took the lead because of selfish motives; there was no public indignation.' Since Li Shih's memorial had included the statement that the people of Wu were gnashing their teeth in profound anger, he avoided ridicule in this way."

61. This is apparently an earlier name for the Ch'ing dynasty Ch'ang 閶 gate, a great gate in the Su-chou city wall near the Wu district yamen. See the map of Su-chou in Su-chou fu chih, vol. 1, pp. 2b-3a.

62. Most sources agree that Chou was escorted out of Su-chou during the second watch of the night of the twenty-sixth day of the third lunar month (April 22, 1626). See Yin Hsien-ch'en, op. cit., p. 21a; and T'i-ch'i chi-lüeh, p. 31b. But Chu Tsu-wen (op. cit., p. 9a) and Chou himself in a letter to Yao Hsi-meng (Chou Chung-chieh kung chin-yü chi, 2.18a-18b) state that he departed in the second watch on the twenty-fifth day (April 21). He arrived at Peking on the twenty-fourth day of the fourth lunar month (May 19). See Yin Hsien-ch'en, op. cit., pp. 21a-21b. Before leaving Su-chou, Chou had considered and rejected the idea of suicide. See Yin Hsien-ch'en, op. cit., pp. 20a ff.; and T'i-ch'i chi-lüeh, p. 31a.

63. The chief Secretariat minister at this time was Ku Ping-ch'ien 顧秉謙 (ca. 1550-1630, chin-shih 1595), whose home was in K'un-shan district, Su-chou prefecture. He retired in 1627 and was erased from the rolls in 1628 after the fall of Wei Chung-hsien. In 1629 the citizens of K'un-shan in an outburst of rage burned and plundered his home, forcing him to flee and spend his last days elsewhere. See MS 306.11a-14a.

64. The secondary minister at this time was Ting Shao-shih 丁紹軾 (1567-1626, chin-shih 1607) of Kuei-ch'ih district in modern Anhwei province. See Kuei-ch'ih hsien chih (45 chüan, 1883 edition), 21.4a-6b.

65. This was Feng Ch'üan 馮銓 (1595-1672, chin-shih 1613), who was among the most venal of Wei Chung-hsien's henchmen and subsequently served under the Manchus. See Shun-t'ien fu chih (131 chüan, 1884 edition), 105.31a-33a; Cho-chou chih (23 chüan, 1765 edition), 14.24a; and biographical notice by Tu Lien-che in A. W. Hummel, op. cit.

66. Cf. HTSL 65.7b-8a.

67. Cf. HTSL 65.16a-17a.

68. A third memorial from Mao I-lu is not recorded in HTSL until the intercalated sixth month (68.25a-25b); it merely reports legal action taken against the leaders of the uprising for imperial confirmation and does not include the statements cited here. A "third memorial" by Mao I-lu is quoted in Li Hsün-chih, op. cit., 3A.36a-36b, together with a reference to an edict about chief rebels who had escaped the net; but this quotation also lacks the statements cited here.

69. T'ien Er-keng was an intimate adherent of Wei Chung-hsien and was given command of the Imperial Guard in 1624. He was in charge of the subsequent persecutions and received many honors and rewards, but after the overthrow of Wei Chung-hsien he was put to death. See MS 306.40a-40b.

70. Fu-yü is the name of an ancient principality of small historical significance located north of China proper. The passage in this text obviously is intended to indicate some rebel who threatened real danger to China's security. It may therefore be a reference to the homophonous Fu-yü 福餘 , one of three Mongol units on China's northern border that harassed the frontier intermittently throughout the Ming period. See MS 328.8a-14a. But it is most likely an oblique reference to the great Manchu chieftain Nurhaci, who during the historical era dealt with in this paper was steadily encroaching on China's northeastern territories. See biographical notice in A. W. Hummel, op. cit.

71. "After the people's uprising, people all were afraid of disaster. There even were some who had previously contributed money (for Chou's cause) and now hurriedly sought to erase their names from the list of contributors." Chu Tsu-wen, op. cit., p. 44a.

72. The catastrophe in Peking on the sixth day of the fifth lunar month (May 31) of 1626 is described in detail in a single-chüan work entitled T'ien-pien ti-ch'ao, which appears in Chieh-yüeh shan-fang hui-ch'ao, in Chih-hai, in Tse-ku chai ch'ung-ch'ao, in Pi-ts'e ts'ung-shuo, and in Huang Yü, op. cit., in the latter case under the title T'ien-pien tsa-chi. It is attributed only to "a visitor in Yen" 燕客 , who Hsieh Kuo-chen (Wan Ming shih-chi k'ao, 5.13b-15a) thinks may be Huang Yü. Further data regarding the event can be found in HTSL 66.6b ff. It is reported that 537 persons died.

73. The Imperial Arsenal was operated by eunuchs. See MS 74.26a.

74. Elephants were maintained at Peking by special troops under the Imperial Guard. See MS 76.8b.

75. Because of the calamity, punishments were suspended through-out the fifth lunar month, but they were resumed in the following month. See Chi Liu-ch'i, op. cit., vol. 1, p. 39.

76. Chou died in prison on the seventeenth day of the sixth lunar month (July 10) of 1626. See Chang Shih-wei, op. cit., p. 13b.

77. The degraded students, whose names actually are not recorded anywhere in this text, were Wang Chieh, Liu Yü-i, Wang Ching-kao, Yin Hsien-ch'en, and Sha Shun-ch'en. All were restored after the overthrow of Wei Chung-hsien. See Chi Liu-ch'i, op. cit., vol. 1, p. 39; and T'i-ch'i chi-lüeh, p. 33a.

78. These five men were put to death in the seventh lunar month (August 22-September 20) of 1626. The people of Su-chou later buried them on the grounds of a temple that had been erected in honor of Wei Chung-hsien by Mao I-lu; and it is said that in 1629 the head of Wei Chung-hsien was brought there and offered in sacrifice to the spirits of the five men. See Chin Jih-sheng, Sung-t'ien lu-pi, 22.30b-35a; Yao Hsi-meng, K'ai-tu shih-mo, p. 15b; and MS 245.7a. Contemporaries considered that Su-chou was fortunate to escape more extensive

punishments and gave friends at court credit for restraining Wei Chung-hsien's fury to such an extent. See Yang T'ing-shu, op. cit.

79. Several sources report other peculiar phenomena. It was said that Ni Wen-huan was visited in broad daylight by the spirit of Chou Shun-ch'ang. See T'i-ch'i chi-lüeh, p. 14a; and Chin Jih-sheng, Wu-jen chuan, p. 30a. It was also said that Mao I-lu died very suddenly when the ghosts of the five commoners similarly called on him. See T'i-ch'i chi-lüeh, p. 33a; and Chi Liu-ch'i, op. cit., vol. 1, p. 39.

80. Cf. MS 245.12a-15b.

81. Cf. Shih-chi (T'ung-wen edition), 55.1a-2a.

# MICHIGAN PAPERS IN CHINESE STUDIES

No. 1, "The Chinese Economy, 1912-1949", by Albert Feuerwerker.

No. 2, "The Cultural Revolution: 1967 in Review", four essays by Michel Oksenberg, Carl Riskin, Robert Scalapino, and Ezra Vogel.

No. 3, "Two Studies in Chinese Literature", 'One Aspect of Form in the Arias of Yüan Opera' by Dale Johnson and 'Hsü K'o's Huang Shan Travel Diaries' translated by Li Chi, with an introduction, commentary, notes, and bibliography by Chun-shu Chang.

No. 4 "Early Communist China: Two Studies", 'The Fu-t'ien Incident' by Ronald Suleski and 'Agrarian Reform in Kwangtung, 1950-1953' by Daniel Bays.

No. 5, "The Chinese Economy, ca. 1870-1911", by Albert Feuerwerker.

No. 6, "Chinese Paintings in Chinese Publications, 1956-1968: An Annotated Bibliography and an Index to the Paintings", by E.J. Laing.

No. 7, "The Treaty Ports and China's Modernization: That Went Wrong?", by Rhoads Murphey.

No. 8, "Two Twelfth Century Texts on Chinese Painting", Shan-shui ch'un-ch'üan chi by Han Cho and chapters nine and ten of Hua-chi by Teng Ch'un, translated by Robert J. Maeda.

No. 9, "The Economy of Communist China, 1949-1969", by Chu-yuan Cheng.

No. 10, "Educated Youth and the Cultural Revolution in China", by Martin Singer.

No. 11, "Premodern China: A Bibliographical Introduction", by Chun-shu Chang.

Price: $2.00 (US) each
Price for Special Issue No. 6: $3.50 (US)
Available from:
Center for Chinese Studies
The University of Michigan
Lane Hall
Ann Arbor, Michigan 48104
United States of America

MICHIGAN ABSTRACTS OF CHINESE AND
JAPANESE WORKS ON CHINESE HISTORY

No. 1, "The Ming Tribute Grain System" by Hoshi Ayao, translated by Mark Elvin.

No. 2, "Commerce and Society in Sung China" by Shiba Yoshinobu, translated by Mark Elvin.

Price: $2.50 (US) each

Available from:

Center for Chinese Studies
The University of Michigan
Lane Hall
Ann Arbor, Michigan 48104
United States of America

Printed and bound by CPI Group (UK) Ltd, Croydon, CR0 4YY

13/04/2025

14656857-0001